Published by Oldie Publications Ltd
65 Newman Street, London W1T 3EG
© 2009 The Oldie

ISBN: 978-1901170-09-2

Printed and bound in the UK by Butler, Tanner & Dennis Ltd

Acknowledgements
The Oldie would like to thank all the writers, illustrators
and cartoonists whose work is reproduced in these pages.

The Oldie
ANNUAL 2010

'Your ideas are outstanding, Beresford. I'm glad I thought of them'

'I haven't seen you at church recently'

 **Welcome to *The Oldie* Annual** for 2010, the third consecutive collection in what will be a regular yearly series.

If you don't know *The Oldie* (founded in 1992) I hope this book will act as a useful introduction to the magazine. Here are samples from many of our regular columnists as well as staple features like Modern and Olden Life (see pages 8–9) and 'I Once Met'.

I would also stress that many of the features and stories reprinted here were unsolicited. *The Oldie*, unlike many of today's magazines, particularly welcomes this kind of material. I hope that readers of this book may feel inspired to try their hand at writing something. I can promise that it will be given careful consideration and – if you're lucky – may actually appear in print!

Richard Ingrams

CONTENTS

26

64

Famous since 1908

24

28

11

72

68

Modern life

What is...
carpaccio?

A MEDIEVAL manuscript records a dialogue between a bishop and his cook, who, when asked to justify his existence, replies to the effect: 'Were it not for me, Sire, you would have to eat your meat raw.' The idea that a bishop would stoop so low as to cook his own food was, of course, unthinkable. The relative social status, not to say earning potential, of the average bishop and celebrity chef has undergone a larger transformation than most in the intervening 700 years, which makes the current vogue for raw meat all the more perplexing.

Every restaurant with aspirations to a Michelin star seems to offer something called 'carpaccio', a dish of thinly sliced raw beef drizzled (another word to set the teeth on edge) with mustard mayonnaise. Carpaccio has been around since 1950, but has only become ubiquitous in the last ten years, largely because, for the restaurant, it is simple and cheap to prepare and, for the diner, it looks and sounds suitably sophisticated. The taste would appear to be of secondary

It is one of those dishes that people tend to order in restaurants but never eat at home – not a good sign

Carpaccio made from thinly sliced sirloin steak

'Your mother's a keen supporter of assisted suicide'

importance. It was invented by Giuseppe Cipriani, the owner of Harry's Bar in Venice, and he named it after the Venetian artist Vittore Carpaccio who, he thought, used a similar colour palette. Carpaccio was a pupil of Gentile Bellini, whose brother Giovanni gave his name to Cipriani's most famous invention, the prosecco and white peach cocktail that is virtually compulsory for American tourists in Venice. Would Vittore be pleased with his new-found fame? It certainly doesn't add anything to an appreciation of his work to realise that the tunic of the lute-playing angel in the altarpiece of the Accademia is the colour of raw beef.

The current fashion is unlikely to last long. It is one of those dishes that people tend to order in restaurants but

never eat at home – not a good sign – and should probably go the same way as steak tartare, an unappetising mixture of minced raw steak and mayonnaise that was briefly popular in the Sixties.

The term carpaccio may last a little longer. It is not unusual to find it attached to goose (not good), venison (worse) or tuna (only slightly better). I recently came across a dish containing a 'carpaccio of cauliflower', which would imply that the word has severed connection with its original meaning and now encompasses anything that is thinly sliced and raw. This is saying more about the pretentions of the restaurant than offering any useful information. How long will it be before we see a carpaccio of cucumber?

BEN MALLALIEU

Olden life

What was...
a list of visitors?

IN THE MIDDLE of the 19th century, local weekly newspapers in holiday resorts and spa towns included lists of visitors who were staying in hotels and boarding establishments within the circulation area of the publication. In fact some weekly newspapers started life simply as a list of visitors, with little more information than coach and rail arrival and departure times and details of religious services. At many resorts, the presence of summer season visitors was one of the major reasons for the establishment of a local paper, and it was quite common for owners of stationery and

It seems strange to us today that readers preferred to read long lists of visitors' names rather than news

printing businesses to be the promoters of these early 'start-ups'.

The summer season ran from around the middle of May until early October, and some of the early weeklies restricted publication to that particular period. A natural development was the late and early visitors lists, which together with more news features and advertising, resulted in the establishment of year-round publication. Some of the earliest local papers to be published all year round were established in towns where there was a proliferation of hydropathic establishments, with constant occupancy irrespective of season.

But what was the point or value of these lists of visitors? It seems strange to us today that readers apparently preferred to read long lists of visitors' names, rather than local or national news. But there was much more to it than that – these lists played an important role in the business and social

mores of the time. Many holiday visitors purchased a list of visitors as they were eager to see who was staying in the town, and where – part of their holiday entertainment being spotting titled visitors or leading dignitaries from their home towns.

From the visitors' point of view, it was pleasing to their vanity and helpful to them in meeting, or avoiding, persons of their acquaintance whilst promenading in the resort or spa. It was an added bonus if they could inform friends that their place of residence contained a satisfactory clutch of Reverends, a doctor or two, a military title, and ideally some addresses containing the magical words 'Park', 'Hall', 'Manor', etc.

Initially, mainly the gentry and aristocracy visited seaside resorts and spas, as early 'lists of visitors' indicate, but as time went on, more clients came from the rising Victorian middle classes – manufacturers, tradesmen, merchants and professionals. For instance, the visitors staying at the Royal Crescent Hotel, Filey, in August 1872 included Their Royal Highnesses, the Grand Duke and Duchess of Hesse and Servants, and Her Royal Highness Princess Louise of Battenberg and Servants. Some 38 years later, however, visitors listed as staying at the same hotel included Captain Gascoigne of the Scots Fusiliers, Charles Gold Esq. of the Middle Temple and Sam Hollins, Esq. of Astley Bridge, Bolton (the last named probably engaged in cotton spinning).

The collation of visitors' names was quite a business, with representatives from the publishers visiting the hotels and boarding establishments on a regular basis. Publishers of the lists were anxious to ensure as many names as possible were included, and new lodging houses and others not visited regularly were requested to send a postcard or to telephone for one of their collectors to

List of Visitors.

Crescent Hotel.

Viscount and Lady Folkestone and suite	Nunappleton, Tadcaster
Lord Lascelles	Harewood House
Captain Brabazone	London
The Hon and Rev the Dean of Windsor	Windsor Castle
Herbert Fordham, Esq Mrs and fam	Odsey, Royston
Major-General Hutchinson	London
Mrs Hutchinson and family	London
Colonel Ford and Party	Hereford Gardens, Park lane, London
G W Alder Esq	Wakefield
William Peach Esq	Hornsey, London
Mrs Peach and fam	do
Charles Gould Esq	Inner Temple
Captain Gascoigne	Scots Fusileer Guards
Wm Greetham Esq	Stainsfield Hall, Lincolnshire
Thomas Greetham Esq	London
Thomas Barber Esq	Huddersfield
Samuel Shepherd Esq	London
— Laforne Esq	Denmark Hill, London
Mrs Laforne and fam	do
Charles Allison Esq	
Mrs C Allison	London
Mrs George Blunt	do
— Farquhar Esq	do
Mrs Farquhar	London
Sam Hollins Esq	do
	Astley Bridge, Bolton

A real list of visitors

obtain a list of their guests.

Anxious to correct any mistakes, the *Bridlington Free Press* stated in 1910, 'The utility of a list of visitors can only be proportionate to its correctness; therefore we will feel obliged if parties observing inaccuracies will give notice to the collector, or to the publishing office, in order that they may be remedied in our succeeding number.'

The publication of lists of visitors ceased in the mid 1950s, although they had been in decline for many years. However, by this time, many of the enterprises had become firmly established as weekly newspapers and, over a period of years, any reference in their titles to being a list of visitors was removed.

With the present-day paranoia about identity theft, when even that voyeurs' delight, the hotel registration book, has disappeared from most reception desks, it is difficult to imagine there was a time when people were quite happy to let everyone know where they were staying on holiday.

ALAN THOMAS

LATEST ARRIVALS

Hotel Barnsley: *Colonel and Mrs Edward Rabbit, Sir Walter Mainwopple, Mr Oswald Thake, Miss Shovel, Mrs Utter and Miss Desdemona Utter, Herr Hugo Schwarnheit, the Hon. Mrs Fudge and Master Eric Fudge, Mrs Nargle and family, Captain Fowlhouse, Miss Nodd, Rear-Admiral Sir Arthur Anymore, Lady Ough, Mr Forbes-Melon, Miss Netta Forbes-Melon, Mr Ulyate A. Niceman and Miss Sukie A. Niceman, Senator Rowle, Mrs Grist, and Mlle Rose Duchanel.*

Hotel Barnsley
Paris

...and a spoof list from 'Beachcomber'

ILLUSTRATION BY HEATH

★ Great Bores of Today ★

'...Hi I'm Zeno and I'll be looking after your table while you eat with us this evening but can I first borrow a few moments of your time to tell you about today's specials for starters we have a roulade of chopped Chinese cabbage and puréed cauliflower on a bed of torn lettuce that's our vegetarian option or alternatively we have a ragoût of crispy duck served with Parmentier sauce and sautéed pine nuts and the soup of the jour is chilled parsnip with a drizzle of chopped oregano and sesame seeds and for the main course can I recommend the monkfish parcels lightly grilled on a fouton of wild rice and then there's the oven-baked belly of pork...'

© **Fant and Dick**

Gilbert Harding

J K RICKARD *recalls an encounter with the larger-than-life but much misunderstood television personality and journalist once referred to as 'the rudest man in Britain'*

At Margate, in 1953. It was party conference time. He'd been lunching with Aneurin Bevan and he kindly offered me a lift back to London in his new chauffeur-driven car.

A signpost for Canterbury moved him, as a good RC, to grumble about the Archdiocese being, as Shaw put it, 'temporarily in the hands of the Anglican heresy'. When I said I'd never seen the cathedral, he told the driver to take us there at once.

On the way, he told me how, as a keen young convert, he had been granted an audience with Pope Pius XII – in French. He began:

'*Priez pour mon père, qui est mort, pas Catholique; pour ma mère, qui vit encore, pas Catholique...*'

A thin voice interrupted him:

'*Tu es converti?*'

'*Oui, Mon Père.*'

'*Sois constant!*'

And that was that...

At the cathedral, he gave me a conducted tour. 'That's where the blessed Saint Thomas was murdered – this is where the bastard Cromwell stabled his horses,' etc. Near the High Altar he overheard a guide say to a visitor: 'You haven't much time. We close at five.'

'We are gathered here today more in celebration of his life than in sadness of his death'

Gilbert exploded. 'What d'you mean – *we close at five?*' he bellowed. 'Is this a pub? *We close at five*! This is the house of God!' He marched off, fulminating.

We paused by the chapel of Saint Benedict. A guide caught up with us. 'The verger would like a word with you, Sir.' 'Tell him I'm here!' roared Gilbert.

To tackle Gilbert in full fury took great courage. The verger had it. He was sorry Gilbert was upset. The cathedral suffered grievously from thieves and vandals, but they could not afford 24-hour security patrols, so with great reluctance they had to close the building overnight. Meanwhile, Gilbert had found the gate of the chapel. 'Even this is closed!'

'For the same reason, Mr Harding. If that were open, there would not be a single hymnbook here by morning... But if you wish to make a prayer to Saint Benedict, I

'What d'you mean – we close at five? Is this a pub?' bellowed Gilbert

will, of course, have it opened for you.'

'Don't bother,' muttered Gilbert, quite defused. Then, in his warmest manner: 'How is your dear dean? I thought he looked very frail last time we met.' The soft answer had turned away wrath and Gilbert and the verger parted amicably.

Back in the car, Gilbert remarked that the episode had reminded him of an encounter between a Roman Catholic cardinal and an American Episcopalian.

'After all, your Eminence, we are both doing God's work, are we not?' said the American.

'Yes, indeed,' murmured the cardinal. 'You in your way – and I in His.'

Donald Sinden

From apprentice joiner to distinguished old stager, the much-loved actor talks to **ALICE PITMAN** *about life, work – and his weekly visits to take tea with Lord Alfred Douglas*

'I DO love nothing in the world so well as you.' Sir Donald Sinden's distinctive mellifluous tones resonate around the empty Bishop's Room of Simpson's-in-the-Strand, where we sit sharing an afternoon pot of coffee. The eulogy is not, I hasten to add, an outburst of passion directed at me, but rather one of many quotations reeled off during the course of an enjoyable few hours in his company. 'Isn't that *beautiful?*' he reflects. 'Could you say it better? Nobody has ever improved on that. Everything Shakespeare said we couldn't say better today. "I love you?" doesn't do it. "Darling, I love you?" – no. But "I do love nothing in the world so well as you" is perfect.'

After more than sixty years as a stalwart of British stage, film, radio and television, nothing has ever supplanted the joy of speaking the words of his beloved Bard. Yet the young Donald had little interest in the theatre. He left school at fifteen and was working as an apprentice joiner when his cousin asked him to take his part in a local amateur production. He was spotted by the director of Brighton's Theatre Royal and asked to join a company that entertained troops returning from Dunkirk. 'I thought he was asking me because I was a genius. It was only later I found out it was because he couldn't get anybody else!' During the war he worked as a joiner

came out, Dirk saying to me, "You know, Donald, they've got it all wrong. *I was there.*" And I felt like saying, "No, Dirk, you were in Pinewood."'

We get on to *Mogambo*, the film he made with Clark Gable, Ava Gardner and Grace Kelly in 1953, and he tells me some amusing anecdotes about the Hollywood legends he has known. I am interested by his lack of awe, and even his scorn, for them. 'Americans, bless their hearts, are so starstruck by film stars, whereas English stage actors don't rate American film actors greatly. They've got no background, whereas our acting goes back to Burbage in Shakespeare's time and it's been passed from generation to generation.'

Indeed, cinema in general comes a poor second to his beloved theatre. 'Films don't interest me. My wife Diana would never let me go with her to the cinema. I'd always be looking at the technical side, the editing, and it would annoy her.' When he played *King Lear* at the RSC in 1977 (winning the *Evening Standard* Best Actor award), a 'charming American gentleman' came to his dressing room to praise his performance and subsequently wrote him a two-page letter of eulogy. 'I took it home to my wife and said "Remember that funny American? Well he's just written me this letter."' 'How lovely,' said his wife. 'It's from Jack Lemmon.' The name meant nothing to him...

yards away from the factory where he worked as a joiner. 'He was virtually living in digs in Hove. I had no appointment. I just went and knocked on his door. He had this gorgon of a housekeeper called Eileen who answered. Then this rather ugly little stooping man appeared. He had a bulbous nose and rheumy eyes and very little hair. To think this was Oscar Wilde's golden boy! I was rather clever. I had swotted up on three of his poems so that when he asked why I was calling on him, I said that I would like to discuss his poetry. Whereas, had I gone in wanting to talk about Oscar Wilde, it would have driven him mad.'

Presumably flattered that a handsome young aspiring actor should call on him, Bosie invited him to tea the following week and so began a series of visits that lasted until his death two years later in 1945. Did Bosie ever mention Oscar? 'He always recalled him with great affection and sometimes his eyes would fill up with tears.' On two occasions, Donald scraped enough money to take him out to lunch at the Pavilion Hotel. Once, a toddler was bawling at another table: 'Portrait of a bloody child,' grumbled Bosie. Donald proffered a drink. 'No, thank you. The wages of gin is breath, as Oscar would have said.'

My afternoon with Sir Donald is great fun. At one point, when talking about the parlous state of modern diction, he shudders with mock rage before suddenly, and somewhat alarmingly, launching into a voice exercise, taught to him as a young man.

'Hip-bath, hip-bath, lava-tory, lava-tory, bi-det, bi-det, DOUCHE!' He repeats it a little louder, his eyes flashing rather wildly. 'Now you say it! Go on!' I make a pitiful attempt and stumble on the second 'hip'. 'HiP!' he enthuses. "HiP-bath! HiP-bath! Punch that P out! Hit it! Make it *explosive!*' Moments later, I'm getting quite good at it. We're happily chanting away together when a waiter walks into the room, looks a bit startled and walks out again ...

He is jolly company as well as a perfect gentleman who pours out my coffee and helps me on with my coat. I do wonder, however, whether his inexhaustible supply of amusing anecdotes and quotations are used to field off more personal probing. A possibility he perhaps acknowledges when I ask if he is acting at the moment. 'What, now?' he jests. 'During this interview? Oh yes, I'm always acting!'

'Hip-bath, hip-bath, lava-tory, lava-tory, bi-det, bi-det DOUCHE!' He repeats it a little louder, his eyes flashing rather wildly. 'Now you say it! Go on!'

by day and performed for the Forces by night, touring Europe and India with ENSA (the Entertainments National Service Association) in 1945.

After the war, he did two seasons at Stratford as well as bit parts in London, alongside such luminaries as Ralph Richardson and Peggy Ashcroft. He was then contracted to Rank films for seven years where he achieved fame starring in many British films of the 1950s, from his debut opposite Jack Hawkins in *The Cruel Sea* to *Above Us the Waves* with John Mills. He rated Hawkins 'a fine actor, both on stage and screen', but found Dirk Bogarde (his co-star in *Doctor in the House*) somewhat elusive. 'He was very much a loner – no one got close to Dirk. He was a bit of a fantasist, too. I remember when the film *Gandhi*

When we met, he was having a break from his one-man tour (*An Evening with... Sir Donald Sinden*), which is produced by his son Marc. His other son, Jeremy, also a gifted actor, died in 1996. 'Losing Jeremy was devastating.' There is a brief, sad silence. 'One expects one's parents to die before you do, not one's children.' His wife Diana died in 2004. 'We were married for 56 happy years. She was my best critic, always totally honest with me.'

As he approaches his 86th birthday, Donald keeps himself busy. He is working on the third volume of his memoirs, as well as penning a little book about Lord Alfred Douglas, the catalyst for Oscar Wilde's imprisonment. During the war, he discovered 'Bosie' – then in his seventies – lived only a few hundred

Memory of the Moor

*Could **BEN MALLALIEU**'s chance encounter with a couple on Saddleworth Moor in the early Sixties have been a lucky escape from the notorious Moors Murders duo?*

I once met Ian Brady and Myra Hindley. Or quite possibly I did nothing of the sort and the people I met were an entirely blameless couple who just happened to be wandering around Saddleworth Moor on a hot afternoon in the early 1960s. It is impossible to tell which. As I grow older it becomes increasingly difficult to be certain about much. Things that once were important no longer matter; quickly forgotten incidents suddenly years later burn brighter.

On that particular afternoon, I was a young teenager staying with my uncle and aunt at Larkwood, the family home, or the latest incarnation of it, the last house on the edge of the wilds. Michael Foot once stayed at Larkwood when he was an undergraduate at Oxford and much later wrote about 'the old Huguenot house in the hills'. But his memory was misleading him and the house he stayed in was then less than forty years old, although it probably looked older. It had been built by my grandparents only at the turn of the century, a deliberately

> *I was busy mending a cattle trough on Saddleworth Moor when I suddenly became aware of two people standing close by, watching me*

grand stone house with a conservatory and fake castellations, a symbol of late-Victorian certainties anticipating an ever more prosperous future which, after the First World War, failed to materialise.

When my grandmother died in 1936, my eldest uncle, who had been planting cotton in Egypt, came home to live in the old house and run one of the family mills. He was a decent, old-fashioned person, a patrician of the old school. When in the 1950s it was rumoured that one of my other uncles might be offered a peerage he was quietly but deeply shocked to learn that someone other that the head of the family could be entitled to call himself Lord Mallalieu.

My aunt found the old house cold and impractical, and most buildings look ugly thirty years after they are built, out of tune with the spirit of the times. Very soon the old house was pulled down and replaced by something that by the time I knew it in the 1960s was itself looking ugly. The general verdict was that the new house was characterless without a single good room, my uncle having hired the local mill architect who was only used to designing factories.

My father, who was the third son, loved the 'old' house. Once playing hide-and-seek with his nephew and niece he found a hiding place they never discovered. Even in the Sixties, when they were grown up, they would ask him where he had been hiding but he said he would never tell them, and he never did, a small secret shared only by him and the old house. Now looking back at what I remember of the new house, I can see traces of *art moderne* in the metal window frames and possibly echoes of Mussolini's North African architecture, understandably ignored for many years but now beginning to be highly regarded.

On the hot summer afternoon in question, I had gone for a walk on my own on the moor and had found a broken cattle trough; the pin holding the ballcock had sheared and the pipe was spraying water over the moor. I was busy mending it with some wire and baler twine when I suddenly became aware of two people standing close by, watching me – I hadn't thought that there had been anyone within a couple of miles.

The woman had blonde hair, possibly dyed, and wore a cotton dress with a floral pattern; the man had neatly combed (possibly Brylcreemed) dark hair and a suit with all three buttons fastened. (Do I really remember this, or is my mind making up facts to fill a vacuum?) I do remember clearly that the woman asked what I was doing and when I explained, she said: 'That's very clever of you,' and then added: 'We're going for a picnic, would you like to join us?' The man said nothing, standing further back, but he seemed to be in control.

I thanked them for the offer but said I had to go home and off I went, and then completely forgot about the incident. The memory remained buried throughout the trial and the subsequent notoriety until one afternoon in 1990 when I was crossing Gray's Inn Road and suddenly, for no particular reason, remembered it all and thought 'Oh'.

TOP CHUMPS

Welcome to *The Oldie*'s card game extravaganza. Simply cut out the Chumps below and glue them to a suitable hard backing. Buy *The Oldie* regularly and you'll be amazed how soon you have a complete set of Top Chumps – ready to do battle with your top CHUMS!!

RICHARD BRANSON

CHUMPFILE

★ Cheesy grin	105%
★ Ballooning fiasco	86%
★ Unreliable trains	60%
★ Manky beard	55%
★ Sleazy ads	13%
★ Knighthood from Blair	60%

CHERIE BLAIR

CHUMPFILE

★ Large Mouth	100%
★ Freebies	97%
★ New-age habits	90%
★ Mad life-coach	95%
★ Ghastly husband	98%
★ Frightful book	100%

JEREMY CLARKSON

CHUMPFILE

★ Road hog	98%
★ Hatred of caravans	90%
★ Global-warming denier	96%
★ Loony crinkly hair	82%
★ Loud voice	95%
★ Laddish jokes	100%

JULIE BURCHILL

CHUMPFILE

★ Funny squeaky voice	105%
★ Porno novel	86%
★ Lesbian affair	60%
★ Stalin worship	55%
★ Defunct magazine	13%
★ Clinically obese	60%

James Michie
24th June 1927 – 30th October 2007

The Oldie's first in-house poet, James Michie's poetry delighted the magazine's readers from 1999 until his death in 2007

Exit, Pursued by a Bear

You'd think by now that the Great Grizzly in question
Through over-eating might have indigestion.
But he ravens on in the chase.
As I dodge through the bad lands
Of old age, I drop behind me baits of honey,
Notes of repentance, promissory money,
Lies, jokes – all useless. When we come face to face,
I shall probably offer to shake hands;
But he'll insist on the full embrace.

Nature Note

The spry jerboa, had he shoes,
Would scorn to put them on his feet,
Although that is the place to choose
If one is trying to be neat.

He'd stuff them with old cabbage leaves
Or dump them in the nearest pond.
No rodent seriously believes
In bounds one may not go beyond.

On Being Fitted with a Pacemaker

What with sex and fags and liquor,
Silly old mulish heart,
Dear unregenerate ticker,
You needed a kick start.

Hey presto! It was done.
Now with my magic inner
Supplementary volt,
Though I'll never be a winner
And can't pass as a colt,
I feel a new urge to run –
For buses, even for fun.

Damnesia

In minimal landslides memory goes –
It's like trying to touch your nose
When you're drunk, and you can't find it.
When it begins, you don't much mind it –
What does it matter, the name of a book or a play,
Or whether it was the day before yesterday

Or last Thursday? But soon
You can't remember where you went on your honeymoon
Or which year it was. When it ends,
You forget the names of old friends
And your own telephone number. But stop fretting
When your retrieval system starts to go rotten.
Just try to remember this: it's better to do the forgetting
Than be the one forgotten.

Seeing Right Through

Once you reach seventy, the wise advise,
View everything as a blessing in disguise.
The snag is, with my eyes, at this late date,
Disguises are damned hard to penetrate.

Nature Note

A politician when disgraced
Might crawl away and hide, you'd think;
Yet spiderlike, flushed down the waste,
He clambers back into the sink.

Collage (being 14 sentences culled from postcards received over the years)

The ears are rather poignant.
Why has no one given Stephen Spender a drink?
I look forward to painting you.
The child you bounced on your knee has written a very, very
    boring book.
My hands are worse this winter.
I'm as happy as a clam.
What is Holman Hunt up to here?
Keep, poet, those erotic visions of yours.
The comforts of philosophy are only for the strong.
How kind of you to respond so promptly.
I love you.
The Bering Sea is hellish swimming.
Mein Gott! Women!

Cancer, or the Biter Bit

I used to fancy crabmeat as a treat:
Now Crab's the epicure, and I'm the meat.

Dog Day Matinees

*When **MAUREEN LIPMAN** appeared in a regional production of Anton Chekhov's best-known play, her neurotic canine co-star was Diva by name and by nature*

I have had the most wonderful time in Chichester playing Charlotta, the governess in Chekhov's *The Cherry Orchard*. The production was generally derided by the critics, but we just got on with being in the best play ever written. We rehearsed for five weeks in Southwark, then packed up clothes, make-up bags and household pets – in my case legitimately, because Diva was to appear as Charlotta's dog – and legged it down the A3 to our digs in the Chichester basin. Once there we would rehearse technically on stage for one week, open to the press on Friday, play for two weeks, close and go home.

On arrival in Bosham Hoe, I started to cough. I took Manuka honey. Then I started to wheeze, so I drank hot lemon. Then I started to sweat, so I opened the windows. Finally, on the first day of the rehearsals, I started to faint. A friend drove me to the nearest doctor where I found myself unable to speak or even breathe properly. It didn't bode well for opening night. Blood pressure dangerously low and a respiratory infection. Bed. Antibiotics. Panic.

'We'll rehearse without you and I'll get you an appointment with our theatre doctor,' said our company manager. After two days in bed, the company doctor declared me a fit woman with a rough chest and splendid blood pressure. So back to the theatre I went, wheezing like a VW exhaust. Alice, my dresser, laced me into a boned corset, layers of heavy clothing, hat and gloves, just in time for the last rehearsal before opening night.

The Chichester Theatre is a Sixties construction with one of the most unforgiving stages on earth. It thrusts out into the auditorium on three sides and the seats leap up from there and embrace it. Entrances are made via several steep flights of steps. Our costumes were long and we all had luggage. I told my baffled Basenji to follow me on and sit and I would give her a treat. She looked doubtful as only a furrow-browed dog can and huddled in the dark awaiting our cue. On a green light, six overdressed actors, two stage managers and a dog all started improvising loudly about trains being late as we climbed and burst forth onto the stage.

My entrance and exit line was 'I give my dog nuts. She likes nuts,' and with the help of a chicken crunch, dog and mistress managed on and off and even got a small 'aah'. The *Express* critic wrote that I'd brought on my own dog to pull focus from the other actors. I wrote to him asking if *Express* owner Richard Desmond's dog would have been less distracting.

Sometimes mixed reviews can bind a cast together and galvanise the show into improving each night. Dame Diana Rigg was valiant. The sun shone, West Wittering beach beckoned, the houses were full and we all relaxed and started the serious business of being in a play out of town – where to eat, who's bringing in the cupcakes and which is the most canine-welcoming pub.

Only Diva showed signs of depression. Her life became weird. Where's my bed? Where's my Hyde Park? And why do I have to go up those stairs every night? By the second week she'd developed squits, a poorly paw and reinvented the hang-dog expression. Two weeks' rest, said the

Chichester audiences accepted a black Labrador in rural Russia with the same aplomb as they'd accepted a barkless dog of the African Congo

vet. Our company manager suggested a week in The Priory with Amy Winehouse's lurcher. It was suggested that I take on a glove puppet in the absence of a dog. I replied that a psychotic governess wasn't in any of Chekhov's early drafts. Instead, I seized Jemma Redgrave's affable black Labrador, Mabel, who had none of Diva's neuroses. In exchange for a handful of Good Boy cookies, she performed to perfection. Chichester audiences accepted a black Labrador in rural Russia with the same aplomb as they'd accepted a barkless dog of the African Congo, and Diva returned for the last few shows with a look of Margo Channing in *All About Eve*.

Our favourite comment on the production was made by two white-haired ladies wearing floral dresses as they left the theatre: 'Well, I thought it was very enjoyable, didn't you, Mary? But why on earth they had to set it in Russia is beyond me.'

ILLUSTRATION BY DAVID STOTEN

scaling
academic heights

My father, Noel Howard Symington, was one of the group of students who scaled the spires of Cambridge in the 1930s. Using the pseudonym 'Whipplesnaith', he recorded these feats in *The Night Climbers of Cambridge,* published in 1937.

IAN SYMINGTON'*s father was one of a group of 1930s Cambridge students who climbed the city's ancient buildings at night. Who said extreme sports were a modern invention?*

This fact was obviously known but infrequently referred to in my family when I was growing up. Equating the quiet, retiring father of my youth with the courageous (or foolish) character who, with fellow students, used the historic Cambridge skyline as a nocturnal adventure playground, was always a stretch.

He is clearly identifiable in many of the photographs, notably those of King's

Chapel (see right). Although none of the climbers ever sustained serious injury, my father suffered severe rope burns to his hands during a descent from the Chapel. His left hand never fully recovered from the rope incident, and was always numb in cold weather.

He was very reticent about those exploits and never revealed to me the names of the other Night Climbers. I know that Wilfred Noyce, part of the 1953 Everest expedition, was a contemporary, but my impression

was that they never climbed together. Unfortunately, I didn't press him about the others, but if any of the climbers or photographers are still alive it would be wonderful to hear from them.

I am especially delighted that Oleander Press has brought out a new edition of *The Night Climbers of Cambridge* as, for over twenty years, I was without a copy. I searched many bookshops, but although everyone knew of the book it had been out of print since 1952. My son Andrew finally found me a copy in the late 1990s.

'The ground is precisely one hundred feet directly below you. If you slip, you will still have three seconds to live'

Reading the book again immediately brought back to me my father's laconic humour and his use of slightly formal yet captivating language. He greatly admired the writing styles of Joseph Conrad and T E Lawrence, and once told me that every word and every sentence should be perfect. To this end, he was prepared to sit and think for as long as it took until the correct words came to him.

Sadly my father died in May 1970 at the age of 56. Rheumatic fever while at school at Rugby had left him with a weak heart, and he never went on to achieve great mountaineering fame. He did, however, climb Mount Kenya on a number of occasions, including an ascent with the first lady and the first black man ever to reach the summit. From the pictures you can see that he obviously had a great sense of balance and a head for heights, coupled with a sense of adventure that would surely have led him to many other exploits had his health been better.

Now, though, we are once again free to read about his most infamous ones.

Facing page, left: cameras, ropes and men

Facing page, right: Nares Craig, later to become a well-known Communist and radical architect, stands triumphantly atop the 'Wedding Cake', New Court, St John's, c. 1936

Above: King's Chapel – 'As you pass round each pillar, the whole of your body except your hands and feet are over black emptiness'

Modern life

What is...
mis-mem?

'Breathtaking, heart-stopping honesty... gives you the best insight I have ever come across' Shy Keenan, Phoenix Survivors

our little
secret

a father's abuse
a son's life destroyed

duncan fairhurs

Please Let It Stop

The true story of my abused childhood

Jacqueline Gold

Toni Maguire

Don't Tell Mummy

A true story of
the ultimate betrayal

THERE WAS A time when travellers seeking to while away a journey might pick an Agatha Christie, or perhaps a Jane Austen. The idea that they might divert themselves with stories of excrement-covered children enduring anal rape or young girls masturbating nuns would seem frankly perverse. Yet it has become more than likely that the person sitting next to you on the 8.15 is reading about children eating their own vomit.

They fuck you up, your mum and dad. But plainly Larkin had no idea what was out there. It has taken the exponential rise of the misery memoir, or mis-mem, for the scales to drop from our eyes. Harper Non-Fiction, the leading publisher in the genre, dresses it up as 'inspirational literature'. Practitioners, and their avid fans on Amazon, call it 'survivors' stories'. Waterstones devote large shelves to 'Painful Lives'. Whatever you call it, the format is instantly recognisable. A pale cover, featuring a weepy or woebegone child, and a cringe-making title such as *Please, Daddy, No* or *Daddy's Little Earner* or *Tell Me Why, Mummy*.

Most observers blame the birth of misery lit on Frank McCourt's 1996 *Angela's Ashes*, followed in 2000 by Dave Pelzer's memoir, *A Child Called It*, in which he revealed an unpleasant childhood at the hands of his alcoholic mother who sent him to clean the bathroom and 'put a bucket, filled with a mixture of ammonia and Clorox, in the room with me and closed the door ...' Pelzer's grandmother commented that, 'His books should be in the fiction section', but *A Child* was a massive seller, spawning two sequels and 3.5 million sales in the UK alone.

From thereon misery deepened like

Behind their rise may lie more repulsive motivations. Most are voyeuristic, some frankly pornographic: many believe they fuel an interest in paedophilia

a coastal shelf, prompting competitive dysfunction. So David Thomas in *Tell Me Why, Mummy* was obliged to 'pleasure' his drunken mother. Stuart Howarth was raped by his own father and forced

'First of all, I'd like to thank my Dad, who sexually abused me, then my Uncle, who beat me up mercilessly, and also my friends, who bullied and humiliated me for so many years'

to have sex with pigs in *Please, Daddy, No*. In *Damaged* Cathy Glass revealed that not only was Jodie, a seven-year-old placed in her care, abused, but within days of moving into the Glass home was masturbating on the sofa and smearing her face with excrement.

To the publishing industry, the mis-mem has brought nothing but delight. By 2007 the sector occupied nine per cent of the British book market, shifting 1.9 million copies a year and generating £24 million revenue, with 80 per cent of sales through supermarkets. Various offshoots have been spawned – the canine misery memoir, which boils down to bad times with a dog, and the celeb mis-mem, such as Clarissa Dickson Wright's *Spilling The Beans* (drunk dad beat her with poker) and Judge Constance Briscoe's *Ugly* (beaten, starved and forced to drink bleach).

Inevitably, as the horrors multiplied, questions of credibility arose. The most dramatic case was that of James Frey whose *A Million Little Pieces* in 2003 was a bestselling account of the prison life of a drug-addicted criminal, abused by a lecherous priest. Perhaps because he had been promoted by Oprah Winfrey, it became a huge story when it emerged that Frey had spent not 87 days in jail, but a couple of hours. The American media went into convulsions about 'trust', 'truth' and 'the contract between author and reader'.

But nobody was really bothered. Other exposés followed, such as that of Kathy O'Beirne's 2005 memoir, *Don't Ever Tell* (tortured by dad, experimented upon in a psychiatric hospital, raped by priests and a policeman before giving birth at 14 in a Magdalene laundry). This tale was hailed as 'so horrific, it is almost unbelievable'. Yet despite widespread questioning of her account, the story became the most successful 'non-fiction' book ever written by an Irish writer.

Some might argue there is nothing

By 2007 the mis-mem sector occupied nine per cent of the British book market

new in this taste for childhood misery. Where would Dickens have been without children to be beaten and starved and locked in cellars? Yet behind the rise in today's degradation tales may lie more repulsive motivations. Most are sordid and voyeuristic, some frankly pornographic: many observers believe they fuel an interest in paedophilia. At the very least, writer and sociology professor Frank Furedi claims, they trade in 'the pornography of emotional hurt', allowing readers to immerse themselves in a world of appalling cruelty that should be kept private.

What mis-mem says about our society is far too depressing to contemplate. Has its ethic seeped into the wider culture, encouraging people to blame their setbacks and inadequacies on the damage wreaked on them by their childhood? Does it add to the lurking distrust of the family unit which already means mothers need clearance from the Criminal Records Bureau before they can change costumes at the school nativity play?

As with all misery-memoirs, however, we can end on a positive note. It seems a dash of real-life misery in the form of the recession has dampened appetites for child abuse horror. In 2008 the mis-mem market dipped badly, with combined sales of the top ten best-sellers down 27 per cent on the previous year. It's sad, of course, for the writers. But something tells me they'll get over it.
JANE THYNNE

Voices from the grave

Every month, Oldie readers send in extracts and quotes from long-ago published books which still have a quite uncanny relevance today...

"The ordinary method of replenishing the Party Funds is by the sale of peerages, baronetcies, knighthoods and other honours in return for subscriptions. The traffic is notorious. Everyone acquainted in the smallest degree with the inside of politics knows that there is a market for peerages in Downing Street, as he knows that there is a market for cabbages in Covent Garden; he could put his finger upon the very names of the men who have bought their "honours".'
From *The Party System* by Hilaire Belloc and Cecil Chesterton, 1911.
Spotted by the Ed

'Shocking fatality at Primary School. Titled Victim. Haymaker's sensational 7.15 pm discovery. Cord round schoolboy's neck. Haymakers working in a field adjoining Sudeley Hall Preparatory School late yesterday evening were horrified to find the body of a boy underneath one of the stacks... The Headmaster, who is also president of the Staverton and District Archaeological Society, in an interview stated that he suspected the crime to be the work of some vagrant, and attributed the wave of violence which has lately been sweeping the country to the disastrous policy of the late Labour Government.'
From *A Question of Proof* by Nicholas Blake, 1935. Spotted by Peter B Reed

'The cause of deaths and injuries is speed, noting that in the centres of large towns, where cars have to go very slowly, because there are so many of them, the casualties are comparatively small. [We must] hope that the number of cars will be so increased that they will be forced to go as slowly on the roads of the country as they do in the centres of our large towns. Perhaps when we all have cars... motoring will stultify itself and cars get wedged into a single stationary block.'
From *Joad's Opinions* by Dr C E M Joad, first published in 1945.
Spotted by John Bourne

'"I said," observed Greenwood, "that the one sort of murder we can't stop is murder by someone like a religious fanatic. That brown fellow probably thinks that if he's hanged, he'll go straight to Paradise for defending the honour of the Prophet."'
From *The Scandal of Father Brown* by G K Chesterton (1929).
Spotted by Caroline Richmond

SHOPPING

*Oldie shopping correspondent **ALICE PITMAN** would rather stick her head in a bucket than spend a morning at toyshop Hamleys*

'STEP INSIDE the loudest, most exciting place in the world!' hollers a drama-student-cum-wizard outside Hamleys flagship store down Regent Street. Meanwhile, a knight-errant and a thing vaguely resembling a dragon accost random shoppers and order them to 'SMILE!'

This retail bullying masquerading as fun is a bit much for a rainy Tuesday morning in November. And do I detect a whiff of desperation in their passive-aggressive cajolery? At the time of writing, Iceland's economy is imploding and it turns out that Hamleys, surprisingly, is owned by one of that country's biggest companies, Baugur. Yet if this world-famous shop, established in 1760 and considered one of London's biggest tourist draws, were to go under, would it really be such a loss?

In its present form, I believe not. This giant toy emporium, which once conjured up Victorian Christmas card images of

> ## The ultimate 'I saw you coming' shop that cynically trades on its historic name

cherubic-faced tots staring in wonder at charming window displays of fairies and wooden soldiers, has been supplanted by six storeys of the kind of over-priced, mass-produced disposable junk you can buy anywhere. And I would strongly question their self-proclaimed boast of being 'the finest toyshop in the world' when most of their stock can be bought pounds cheaper at rival stores. Even traditional board games like Scrabble and Monopoly, and quality wooden toys such as Brio, are as much as £5 less a piece at places like Toys Я Us, The Entertainer and Argos. In fact, Hamleys is the ultimate 'I saw you coming' shop that cynically trades on its historic name in order to rip off naïve Americans, perma-tanned Euro-

trash and hapless British shoppers alike.

I could forgive paying the few quid extra if they offered a unique and rewarding shopping experience. But they don't. Hamleys is a cramped and shabby disappointment, with piped chart music blaring out from their in-house radio and nowhere comfortable to sit while your children wander down aisles of Barbies and Lego Bionicles, searching for that elusive toy of their dreams. And if you are not ducking the remote-controlled helicopters and boomerangs operated by wacky employees who call everyone regardless of age or gender 'you guys', you're being pestered into watching a demonstration of multi-coloured blow pens (and it's always the same picture of a rainbow): 'Exclusive to Hamleys, you guys, so enjoy!' You smile weakly and despise yourself for parting with £20 when you know you could probably purchase something pretty similar for a fraction of the cost somewhere else. 'Thank you for playing with us!' reads the whimsical sign emblazoned above the exit. Even the way they forgo the use of anapostrophe in their name annoys me. On my way out, the wizard is still at it: 'Everyone loves Hamleys!' he exclaims to no one in particular.

Not me, matey.

'We had a tree last year, but this year we've gone for decking'

EXPAT
DONALD TRELFORD

Mallorca, Spain

MY SPANISH teacher has sacked me. Lucy was too polite to put it like that, but her meaning was unmistakable: 'Why don't you take a break for a while?' I don't blame her really. She wasn't fooled. Every week, an hour before seeing her, I would go to a coffee bar and mug up the previous lesson, but I'd do nothing in between. I console myself with the thought that I simply lack the gift of tongues. I read a John Grisham thriller in which a guy on the run taught himself Italian. 'I'm fifty,' he says, 'that's too old to learn a new language.' There you are, I said to myself, and you're a couple of decades further down the line.

My problem is that I'm tongue-tied in a foreign language unless I can see the words in my head. A friend here, a former civil servant, is the opposite. He plays golf and mixes with the Spanish caddies (from whom he learns some fruity expressions). He plunges in bravely in Spanish, making it up as he goes along, and it seems to work splendidly. I haven't the nerve for that. It doesn't help that on Mallorca they speak a mix of Catalan and orthodox Castilian Spanish. For example, if you say *gracias* (thank you) as you leave a shop, you're likely to receive a hissed *gracis* in response. Some police and council officials have signs up saying they refuse to talk in English. In general, though, one is humbled by the fact that so many of the locals speak our language; that doesn't happen in the UK.

The irony is that I'm a bit of a hard-liner on immigrants speaking English in Britain. I remember getting in quite a lather once at my doctor's in Islington when I was handed a pamphlet in twenty-one languages. I stormed into the GP saying: 'Why do you do this? Not only does it cost a fortune in translators, but it actively discourages them from learning English and becoming part of our community.' Yet here I am, after five years in Spain, barely able to order a meal, no different really from the fat, red-faced *Daily Mail* readers who shout loudly at the locals in English.

It's that rather ghastly image that stops me giving up. If you live in someone else's country, it seems only decent manners to try to talk to them, even if it's only a brief, polite exchange with the newsagent or garage mechanic. The woman at the laundry insists that I talk Spanish and patiently coaxes out a few phrases like a teacher with an infant learning to read. Some friends tried to improve their language skills by going into the mountains and speaking only Spanish to each other all day. 'How did it work out?' I asked. 'We had long, silent walks.'

Miles Kington
Oldie columnist 1992–2008

Always on my mind

Some sex advice I've never forgotten...

Memory is not always there when you want it. My wife suddenly said to me yesterday, 'What is the name of the young female character in *Great Expectations*?' and of course I could remember Pip's name and Miss Havisham's and Magwitch's (though not Joe's) but I couldn't for the life of me remember Estella. (Yes, I've looked it up now, although I don't suppose I'll ever need the knowledge again.)

But it works the other way round. Memory is often there when you don't need it. For instance, in 1962, during my second and last long university vacation, I played in a jazz trio in Spain, near Algeciras, for two months, and while I was there I was told two supposedly typically Spanish jokes, which I can remember in detail to this day. Why, when I have forgotten so many since?

I can remember a sign I saw on a shop door in Gibraltar. It said: 'Closed due to the death of a member of the family in India.' What has made that stick in my mind?

I can remember during the same Andalucian holiday making friends with the crew of a Carol Reed film being shot nearby, *The Running Man*, and I can remember the cameraman saying to me that in all the films he had worked on, he had only ever met one director who, at a pinch, could do the job of all the people on the crew. Cameraman, soundman, actor, writer, director, he could do it all. Know who it was? He bent closer, as if it were a secret. 'Peter Ustinov,' he said.

This is a conversation that took place over forty years ago, and I can still remember it, even though I can't remember the cameraman's name.

Why do things like this stick in the memory? And why do I remember equally clear snapshots from New York, two years previously? In 1960, spending what would now be called a part of a gap year before going to Oxford, I worked for three months in New York. And there one day I met and made brief friends with a young man called Dick Volpe.

We met, I believe, at some sort of political gathering, perhaps something to do with that year's Presidential election (Nixon v. Kennedy), and got talking, and went for a drink. He was studying psychology. I was going to do languages. We were young. We interested each other.

He said to me: 'How's your sex life?'

Well, I didn't really have a sex life.

I hadn't lost my virginity yet. Being a fresh-faced, not unattractive young man, I was constantly approached by gay New Yorkers who would very much like to

We were young. We interested each other. 'How's your sex life?' Dick Volpe asked me

have relieved me of it, but I was too innocent, I think, to even realise the temptations being held out to me and I remained an effortless virgin.

'I don't actually have a sex life yet,' I said. 'I think I'll wait till I really fall in love with a girl, and then we'll see what happens.'

'Oh, for God's sake!' said Dick Volpe. 'Don't be stupid! You mustn't do that! That's madness! That's the old romantic delusion! You can't wait till then – you've got to go ahead with it now! Have sex

I TOLD YOU THERE WERE NO F✗✗✱ING FISH IN THIS BLOODY POND!

now and then you'll be ready when love comes along!'

I was very struck by this. I must have been struck, to have remembered this conversation and his name forty years on. No, forty-five. This guy, remember, was studying psychology, so to my untutored mind he must have known what he was talking about. Alas, I cannot really say I followed his sensible advice.

I managed to lose my virginity the next year, 1961, back in England, to a woman almost twice my age, which was so delightful that I don't think I got round to having any sex again for another two years or so, and then it wasn't nearly so delightful when I did...

Enough. And yet, even now, I sometimes daydream and start wondering whatever happened to Dick Volpe. Indeed, I once did something about it.

I put his name into Google, and I found that there was a Dr Richard Volpe running a child psychology unit in Toronto. Same name! Psychology! That must be the guy! Excitedly, I emailed and then wrote to him, telling him that I had cherished his advice on sex all these years. Coolly and calmly, he wrote back: 'Hi! I received your letter today and had gotten the email mentioned. The person you met in NY isn't me because I never left Ohio until the 1970s en route to Alberta. Also, I am not Dick Volpe: that was my Dad who died long before the 1960s. I applaud your search efforts and wish you luck in the future. All the best.'

I think that maybe I am doomed not to find Dick Volpe again, and I think maybe it is for the best, because if we did meet again, what would we talk about after we had talked about the first steps in teenage sex, a subject which has totally lost its charm for me over the years?

On the other hand, if Dick Volpe should happen to read this after all those years, I wouldn't mind if he got in touch. After all, he might by now have some tips on the last steps in middle-aged sex to pass on to me.

Famous since 1908

Poop-poop!

100 years of Mr Toad

The Wind in the Willows has given enormous pleasure to generations of readers. In 2008 **RICHARD INGRAMS** celebrated its centenary – and examined the sad life of its author, Kenneth Grahame

Kenneth Grahame
in 1912, drawn by
John S Sargent

Illustration by Robert Geary

For a fictional all-male group of Thames Valley idlers, stemming from the imagination of a senior Bank of England official, to survive from the Edwardian age into the politically-correct world of the 21st century is an extraordinary achievement. But that is what they have done – Mole, Ratty, Badger and Toad, the cast of *The Wind in the Willows*, first published in 1908.

Not only have they survived, they have flourished through a series of editions selling thousands upon thousands of copies, not to mention stage shows and films. And they will still be here, I predict, when Harry Potter is forgotten.

Like many of the world's bestsellers, *The Wind in the Willows* was turned down by at least one publisher and received a fairly lukewarm reception from the critics when it was eventually published. 'As a contribution to natural history,' the *Times*'s anonymous reviewer wrote, 'the work is negligible ... Grown-up readers will find it monstrous and elusive.'

Seeking to explain the later success of the book, Grahame's biographer Peter Green claimed, rather too seriously, that 'Its symbolism embodies mankind's deepest and most ineradicable yearnings: the pastoral dream, the Golden Age, the search for lost innocence.' None of that has much to do with Grahame's most famous creation, Mr Toad, who makes such a special appeal to children and without whom the book would be colourless and bland.

Toad is the archetypal boaster, megalomaniac and monster. He is Jeffrey Archer, Robert Maxwell, Alan Clark – but with one very important difference. He is, as Grahame intended him to be, a loveable figure and, in his way, a kind of hero. Significantly, at the end of the story, Mr Toad remains a free man when by rights he would have been recaptured and put back in prison. More importantly, he has no intention of mending his ways. 'Of course Toad never reformed,' Grahame once wrote. 'He was by nature incapable of it.'

Attempts have been made to trace the inspiration for Mr Toad, with many rather absurd theories put forward. Some claimed he was based on Horatio Bottomley, the Robert Maxwell of his day. Alan Bennett, who adapted *The Wind in the Willows* for the stage, even saw Grahame as an anti-semite and Toad a vicious caricature of a Jewish financier. More convincingly, it has been suggested that Toad was inspired

Toad is the archetypal boaster, megalomaniac and monster. But he is, as Grahame intended him to be, a loveable figure

in part by Grahame's only child, his son Alastair, for whom the book was originally composed in the form of bed-time stories. Spoiled and bumptious, Alastair showed Toad-like tendencies. Grahame's relationship with the small boy was the only truly happy one he had. His mother died when he was only five. His father, Cunningham Grahame, a Scottish lawyer and an alcoholic, sent away his four children to be brought up by their grandmother in England. His wife Elspeth was hopelessly neurotic and, most tragically of all, Alastair, who had been born half-blind and had always been 'difficult', committed suicide on a railway line in Oxford when he was only 19.

Grahame's characters can be seen as creatures bred out of this unhappy background. They are all bachelors with a special love for their homes. As a young man Grahame had had a recurring dream of a room of his own somewhere in London, a dream so vivid that he actually scoured the city for days in the hope of finding his room. 'A certain little room – very dear and familiar, sequestered in some corner of the more populous and roaring part of London – always the same feeling of a homecoming, the world shut out, of the idea of encasement.' The story echoes the most powerful passage in the book, when Mole, walking through the snowy night with Rat, is suddenly overcome with homesickness: 'Now with a rush of old memories, how clearly it stood up before him in the darkness. Shabby indeed and small and poorly furnished, and yet his, the home he had been so happy to get back to after his day's walk. And the home had been happy with him, too, evidently and was missing him and wanted him back...'

Grahame never found his dream room in London. The nearest he came to the feeling of peace and security it promised was by writing his famous book – 'the world shut out' – and so finding not merely success, which he was uncomfortable with, but happiness of a sort and the 'encasement' that he craved.

HELEN BAMBER *has spent her life working on behalf of the violated. Now in her eighties, she continues to support survivors, helping them rebuild their lives. Interview by* MELANIE McFADYEAN

Bearing witness

Helen Bamber is poised, humorous, welcoming. She is used to being interviewed; her reputation as a champion of human rights spans the world. She has received many awards – European Woman of Achievement in 1993, an OBE, an award for a Lifetime's Achievement in Human Rights in 1998, honorary doctorates, degrees from half a dozen universities. But there is another kind of testament to her work, one that can't be hung on a wall, lodged in the memories of thousands of people who remember her as someone who listened while they told her of their experiences of torture, rape, murder, human trafficking, genocide.

She isn't worthy or self-satisfied; she creases up with laughter, likes a bit of a gossip. She is always beautifully turned out, hair and make-up perfect. 'I'm very interested in clothes, make-up and hair – it's a part of my defence. If I have a difficult telephone call to make I comb my hair or put my lipstick on.' This stylishness comes from her mother who, as the bombs were falling, would make sure she was elegantly dressed before going to the air raid shelter in the garden of their home in North London.

She turned 84 in May 2009 but it seems meaningless. She's at work by 7.30. She lives on her own; 'I lead such a crazy life that nobody would put up with it for very long.' She has two sons and one young grandchild. She and her husband Rudi,

a Jewish refugee from Nazi Germany, parted many years ago. 'I have immense energy, more now than when I was young. I need less sleep and can work a seven-day week. I feel one day it'll go whuff! and I'll be on the floor and it'll all be over.'

Her parents were Jewish of Polish descent, and her father, obsessed with the Nazi threat, would read to her from *Mein Kampf* or articles by Goebbels. As a child she feared the Nazis would invade and she and her family would be eliminated. She grew up with the miasma of persecution familiar to many Jewish children, perhaps the source of her capacity for compassion.

> *Thousands of people remember her as someone who listened while they told her of their experiences of torture, rape murder, human trafficking and genocide*

It was to be crystallised by her first job when, at twenty, she worked with survivors at Bergen Belsen in Germany, shortly after liberation.

Back in the UK she was appointed to the Committee for the Care of Young Children from Concentration Camps, working for the welfare of 722 young children and adolescents suffering from the effects of violence and loss. She worked in collaboration with the Anna Freud Clinic. She then took a number of hospital posts before joining Amnesty International. In 1985, she and others established the Medical Foundation for the Care of Victims of Torture. In 2005 she left and set up the Helen Bamber Foundation, which offers medical consultation, therapeutic care, human rights advocacy and practical support to survivors of human rights violations. They help some 1,600 asylum-seekers and refugees from more than 70 countries.

Her office is light and welcoming. We sit at a small round table. On it is a bowl of smoothly polished stones. 'Some people I see really cannot speak and we talk about very simple things that have nothing to do with what has happened to them to help them to communicate with me. We'll begin sometimes with the stones. I will ask them to take a stone and hold it, then I will hold it and then I will give it to them: it's this awful phrase in the trade, a transitional object, something from me to them.' Her voice is soothing, slightly husky, her delivery mesmeric.

From early childhood life threw experiences at Bamber which drew her further into the person she became – a witness, a listener, her unsentimental empathy never dimmed. She remembers a woman clutching her and desperately rasping out her story just after the war. She said: 'I cannot bring back the dead but I can be your witness. Your story will be told.' When she came back from Germany having witnessed the immediate aftermath of the Holocaust, she was driven by a 'need to bear witness to man's cruelty and inhumanity, the banal cruelty that we see sometimes in our own society. That has stayed with me.'

We talked about the UK's ten immigration detention centres where some 2,500 asylum-seekers, including families with children, are locked up indefinitely without charge. Most of us know little about these places out of which come reports of hunger strikes, self-harm, suicide and neglect. Bamber and her team hear detainees' horrifying stories which most of us would choose to walk away from.

Bamber is rarely sad, more often angry, a slow-burning anger, no ranting or swearing. The anger gives her energy. So when she fell silent and cried, it seemed we should abandon the interview. She said nothing for some time and then spoke for twenty minutes seamlessly, in her slow deliberate way, picking her words with care, editing herself as she goes along – 'No, I didn't mean it quite like that, change that.'

She talked about asylum-seekers whose claims have been rejected and who are living rough, of people whose claims failed partly because 'when you've been violated, you're in shock and you can't speak about what torture really is – the threat to one's sexuality, about lying in your excrement and your urine, screaming, begging for them to stop, you can't talk about that. So you say, "They beat me." And that word beat doesn't sound so bad.

'It's about violating a woman and laughing at her plight and that woman being unable to say what happened to her because most women find it difficult to talk about rape. It's about a woman who's been subjected to female genital mutilation and when they rape her they split her open with a knife in order to enter her because she's sewn up. Women and men can't speak about these things, so they don't give an easy account

of themselves.' Bamber wonders why many officials charged with the responsibility for making informed decisions with such damaged people 'have not been trained in the sensitive facilitating manner in which you can really identify trauma. Is it perhaps that they don't want to identify it? Is it perhaps that it is easier not to hear about these things?'

She talks of people whose stories are 'catalogues of banal neglect, lack of understanding and compassion'. With everything stacked against them, her many clients say they don't know why they go on living, they've lost their families, their homes, everything. 'And then somehow through our therapeutic relationships, together we find reasons for them to go on living.'

Her sadness, she said, came from thinking of the continuum of that banal neglect and abuse of human rights. 'At the end of the war when all the human rights covenants and declarations were being fashioned we had hoped a new world had been born. It was perhaps naïve. I was young at the time and many of us felt a sense that there was now a framework for the protection of those who had suffered at the hands of others – international agreements about violence, atrocity, torture and genocide.'

Helen Bamber, Belsen, 1945

That global ethic dependent on a collective sense of compassion has, she says, to be recreated by successive generations. 'Each generation has to fight for its morality, its compassion and to be able to help people to whom they owe nothing. I listen to people talking about asylum-seekers and refugees and I sense danger; it doesn't take much more to cross the boundary into hatred and violence. I have to keep saying to the public, walk in their shoes.'

She feels encouraged when she visits schools and universities, and meets students who ask intelligent questions. 'I'm not without hope, I've seen people can make change. But it is such a painstaking exercise. I can see where we as an organisation have been able to change lives and change decisions.'

When you have been with Helen Bamber, you leave with a feeling that if more of us had her qualities, the world would change and be a much better and less cruel place.

- **To find out more about the Helen Bamber Foundation, visit** *www.helenbamber.org*
- **To donate skills or money to the Foundation, please contact Elizabeth Super on** *020 7631 4492* **or** *elizabeth@helenbamber.org*

Looking for a safe seat

Staunch supporter of public transport, **TONY BENN** *has come up with an idea to take the strain out of waiting for buses*

It may seem strange that after 51 years in Parliament – which I left in 2001 – I should still be looking for a safe seat. At any airport lounge, railway station or bus stop you will always find people standing about waiting with suitcases or wearing backpacks and showing signs of exhaustion. I come in that category and, having an inventive mind, I decided to design some equipment to make travelling a bit easier.

I consequently came up with two very successful devices that I named the

This article is an appeal to an imaginative manufacturer to mass produce my devices for the public

'seatpack' and the 'seatcase'. The seatpack is a simple backpack on wheels with an extending handle, which I adapted to attach a stool. When it is on the ground, you pull out the stool and sit in reasonable comfort. The seatcase is based on a conventional suitcase with wheels and an extending handle. I bought a canvas shopping trolley with a seat, removed the canvas bag and attached the suitcase to the frame.

The photographs, above and right, show how these two systems work and, having used them myself, I can recommend them.

This article is an appeal to an imaginative manufacturer to mass produce them for the public; I can tell you now that I

will be a guaranteed customer, not only for myself but for my elderly friends.

If I were a young entrepreneur, I would patent the travelling seat ideas myself, set up a small business to manufacture them and advertise them as 'Tony Benn's Safe Seats'. Being a great believer in public services I would be happy if the main benefit went to those who would appreciate them most.

I am grateful to *The Oldie* for agreeing to publish this. It's a favourite magazine of mine and I especially like the advertisements, which cater for every known need of my generation.

If you are a manufacturer interested in producing my travel seat designs and would advertise them in *The Oldie*, write to me care of *The Oldie* or email: **theoldie@theoldie.co.uk**.

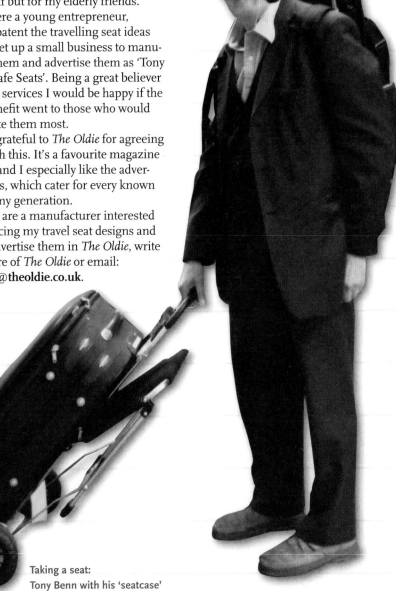

Taking a seat:
Tony Benn with his 'seatcase'

The world according to
Enfield Snr

Why do the Freemasons not want me?

A number of interesting and possibly exciting things have failed to happen to me in my life. At least, I think they would perhaps have been interesting and perhaps exciting if they had happened, but as they didn't I cannot of course be sure.

Most of all, no one has ever asked me if I would like to be a Freemason. I wonder what it is that marks me out as so obviously not Freemason material. They are, one knows, a secretive organisation, but they are not as secretive as all that. I still get my old school magazine and it publishes, or until very recently used to publish, notices of meetings of the Old Westminster Lodge. Real secret societies do not do that. There is never a notice of a meeting of the Old Westminster branch of Opus Dei telling us how Ruth Kelly has been elected branch president. If there is such a branch, and if she is president (which she is bound to be, if it exists), they keep it under wraps, whereas the Masons come out bold as brass, but never ask me if I would like to join.

I have to say, I find this hurtful. Old Westminsters, or Old Wets as we are known in the fraternity, give each other the tap on the shoulder or the nod and the wink, or whatever it is they do, and never once come anywhere near me. I like to have a go at things which are within my ability, and really believe that being a Freemason is something I could do reasonably well. As far as one knows, Freemasons roll up one trouser leg, put on funny aprons and repeat special formulae which they have learned by heart. I feel confident that I could manage that and being, as they say, definitely up for it, I cannot but feel aggrieved that I have never been allowed to try.

Naturally my motive for wanting to join is that Freemasonry is said to be a sure-fire way of getting on in the world, which would have been both interesting and exciting if it had happened. I can think of a couple of jobs that I did not get which I bet I would have got if I had given the Masonic handshake to the chairman of the interviewing panel. Possibly all one needs is to master the handshake without bothering with that trouser leg business, but there may be other secret signs that one ought to give in the course of the interview, just to back up the handshake, and I would like to do the thing properly.

No one has ever asked me if I would like to be a Freemason. I really believe that it is something I could do reasonably well

Freemasons are, it is said, wholly or largely devoted to the admirable cause of giving a leg up to other Freemasons, and the police service is full of them, which is yet another reason for joining oneself.

I was told by an ex-copper that he once arrested someone for drink driving and handed in the charge sheet to the duty sergeant who tore it up as the drunk in question was a member of the same Lodge as himself. From which it is obvious that anyone thinking of taking up a life of crime should become a Freemason by way of insurance.

Neither have I ever been headhunted. Nobody has ever wanted my head, which is another source of disappointment.

I had a neighbour who was a headhunter, but he never showed the least inclination to hunt me. He did, however, kindly certify on the necessary form that I am a fit person to own a shotgun, but he gave his profession as 'retired'. 'Retired what?' asked a policeman at the end of a telephone. 'Headhunter,' said my wife, so I believe I may be the only man allowed to use a gun on the say-so of a man who, for all the police knew, spent his working life chopping off the heads of natives in the forests of New Guinea.

Ah well, it is all too late now, but if you want to know what Freemasonry can do for a man, look at Bill Clinton. He went to the same college as the Editor and me, where they tell me he figured as a complete nonentity. He neither took a degree nor made any contribution whatever to the college, so that when he became Governor of Arkansas no one but the college porter had the least idea who he was. The only way washouts like that can get on as he did is obviously by going about Arkansas and Congress giving out secret handshakes, rolling up his trouser leg and prancing about in an apron. If there is another explanation I cannot imagine what it could be.

Good morning! My name's Julian and I'll be your torturer today!

What a piss artist!

Thirty years ago **DAVID STAFFORD** had a rather too-close-for-comfort encounter with the artist and 'drop-out' **RALPH RUMNEY**. He's still not quite over it...

At the tail end of the Sixties, I was sharing a flat on the edge of Bloomsbury with a couple of friends. 'Dropping out' was still in fashion but fading fast; in reality it meant people dropping in and staying too long with their smelly sleeping bags on the living-room floor. One night, Julie (at least that's what I shall call her here) brought home a roughly handsome man with an impeccable accent and easy charm. 'This is Ralph,' she announced, firmly. 'He'll be staying a few days. He's an artist.' It turned out, too, that he was in trouble. He'd been married to Peggy Guggenheim's daughter, Pegeen, and had enjoyed an exotic life in Venice and Paris until she committed suicide. The grief-stricken Peggy had blamed Ralph for the death and set the police and private investigators on to him. He was now lying low in London until the fuss died down. Pretty fascinating stuff, I thought, and felt glad to help.

Several weeks on, however, and my patience was badly fraying. Ralph's capacity for drink was impressive, and combined with Julie's love of throwing gargantuan dinner parties for his circle of artistic friends, they had transformed our small kitchen into a lethal no-go zone. The sink was a mountain of filthy plates and the table a wasteland of empty bottles, dirty wine glasses and stinking cigarette stubs. Meanwhile, behind their door each morning, I would hear Ralph snoring blissfully away. I never once saw him paint a canvas or do anything useful at all. He was the ultimate drop-in nightmare. But because of his troubles, I held my tongue.

Until, that is, one unforgettable night. In the kitchen, as usual, Ralph was trying heroically to solve the problem of Europe's unprecedented wine lake. In my room, fast asleep, I was having a dream about a warm tropical waterfall splashing around my ankles. The noise got louder and louder and suddenly I woke up. I

The Change, 1957, by Ralph Rumney. Tate Gallery, London 2009 ©

switched on the bedside light and there was Ralph, blinking and swaying and having a piss that seemed to go on for ever and ever, all over my bed and on to the carpet. He took no notice of me at all and, when he'd finished, shook himself dry and lurched out of my room.

Ralph's capacity for drink was impressive. I never once saw him paint a canvas or do anything useful at all

The next morning, after I'd cleaned myself up, stripped the bed and rolled away the carpet to be sent to the cleaners, I left a note for Julie asking her to remove him immediately from the scene – and to her credit, she did. I never saw or heard of Ralph again and life moved on through the next three decades.

Then, three years ago, I opened my newspaper and there was Ralph, gazing at me from a photograph that accompanied a generous obituary of him. It brought the

memories flooding (as it were) back.

Ralph Rumney, it turned out, had been a celebrity in 1950s avant-garde circles in London and had even been under contract to the Redfern Gallery, which once a week would send round its chauffeur in a Bentley to pick up his paintings. In a big group show organised by the gallery in 1957, featuring such distinguished British artists as Patrick Heron, Ralph was given the whole ground floor to himself. He was only in his mid-twenties. One of his paintings from this period, *The Change*, was later purchased by the Tate.

But Ralph's brilliant future was quickly behind him. As one of life's natural and untameable rebels, he disdained success and had an uncanny knack of throwing everything away, including his paintings. The son of a miner-turned-vicar, who'd once shared a bed with Keir Hardie when the famous labour leader stayed in Durham, he'd got hooked on the thrill of the forbidden early in life. Aged fifteen, he'd been denounced as a pervert by the Bishop of Leeds for ordering the collected works of the Marquis de Sade from his local library in Halifax, West Yorkshire. He then turned down a place at Oxford, quit art school, and joined the Young Communist League. For a while the historian E P Thompson took him under his wing and tried to educate him in the subtleties of Marxism. But he quickly rebelled against that as well.

What Ralph really liked doing was hanging out with other artists in cafés and bars, and generally living on the edge. He spent most of his life in various European cities rubbing shoulders with such artistic oddballs as William Burroughs, Yves Klein, Marcel Duchamp, Georges Bataille, and Max Ernst. One week he was in Paris, the next in Milan, or Trieste, or Brussels. He also acquired a legendary capacity for drink which earned him the sobriquet 'the Consul', after the alcohol-soaked protagonist of Malcolm Lowry's novel, *Under the Volcano*. But one of his biggest claims to fame, it transpired, was as a founding member of the Situationist International (SI).

Dreamed up at a meeting in 1957 of Ralph's friends in an obscure Italian village, the SI was a heady mix of Surrealism, Dadaism, Marxism and Anarchism. It wasn't always easy to get a handle on it. 'Can you explain what Situationism is all about?' asked a bemused spectator after a presentation by its leading exponent, Guy Debord, author of the key Situationist text, *The Society of the Spectacle*, at the ICA in 1961. 'We're not here to answer c***ish questions,' replied Debord (albeit in French), before storming out in a huff. But the basic idea was that capitalism had reduced everyone to a passive spectator of life, and that liberation could only come through creating 'situations' that disrupted the mundane. Its moment of glory came in May 1968 in Paris when the revolting students adopted its slogans to demand the organisation of chaos.

By then, however, Ralph had moved on. Hardly a year after the founding meeting he was expelled from the SI for having failed to produce a promised psycho-geography of Venice. Yet the city of dreams offered ample compensation and soon he was married to Pegeen and hardly short of a bob or two. But that didn't last long, either, and a decade later he was

again on the road. After our unfortunate encounter in London, he returned to Paris, worked for a while for French radio, hung around with old friends, and then settled down in Manosque in southern France with his cat, Borgia, where he died of cancer in 2002, aged 67. After his funeral in Montparnasse, a group of friends retired to his son Sandro's flat for a few drinks. As they were ready to leave, a sudden gust of wind blew open the windows. 'It's Ralph,' said his son, 'come to get the last of the wine.'

'Flee the ruins, and don't cry in them' was the epigraph he chose for a book of interviews published the year Ralph died. I've since read it, along with a short biography published the same year. They make fascinating reading. He was obviously endowed with acute intelligence and his comments on art are perceptive. No one who admires the paintings of Malevich or Balthus can be just written off. Was this really the drunk who'd pissed on my bed? Or had I just imagined the whole thing?

Then I discovered that amongst his many exploits, Ralph spoke of one with particular relish. In Brussels for a Situationist exhibition, he'd got rolling drunk with some students from the university and they'd led him to the Manneken Pis. This, for those who don't know, is the statue of a little boy pissing into a fountain, and it's Brussels' answer to Rome's Trevi Fountain (which tells you quite a bit about the Belgian capital and maybe the European Union). Anyway, by the time Ralph got there in the early hours of the morning, he'd downed quite a few litres of Belgian beer and his bladder was full, and... Well, yes, you can guess the rest. Ralph pissed on the Manneken Pis and thirty years on was still chuckling over the memory. What a spectacle, what a situation!

So, no, I don't think I imagined the whole thing. It was obviously a pattern in Ralph's life.

So was his wandering. His biography contains a quote that sums up his life: 'I think the trick, as far as possible,' Ralph said, 'is to be sort of anonymous within this society. You know, to sort of vanish.' I'm pleased to think that I once helped him on his merry way.

RANT

I SPY RAMBLERS! There is surely no more annoying sight to the contented countryman than that of a bevy of ramblers proceeding purposefully along their chosen path like a herd of silly sheep.

Twenty or thirty of them perhaps, and all got up in the regular rambler kit: anorak, bobble hat, thick woolly socks drawn up over their trousers and bulky boots from Millets. The keener ramblers may have little canvas sachets dangling round their necks containing the relevant section of the Ordnance Survey map. You would think they were on an expedition to the Himalayas.

Walking is ideally a solitary pursuit – even a single companion can easily become irritating for no very good reason. We should emulate the poet Wordsworth

who 'wandered lonely as a cloud'. Where is the pleasure of traipsing through the fields with thirty pretty boring-looking people in bobble hats?

Nowadays ramblers are not only boring-looking. They have become quite aggressive with their Ramblers' Association campaigns for the Right to Roam wherever they like.

It is a pointless crusade because, such is the lack of farm workers in a countryside run by machines, you can ramble pretty well anywhere you like without seeing a human being and getting accused of trespass.

Of course if you go around with thirty other people in anoraks you could well be resented by farmers who would be more than justified in releasing a few bulls to give you a nasty fright.

RICHARD INGRAMS

What the Papers Say read-through c1980, from left to right: Michael Ryan (producer); Ann Leslie (presenter); Jan Elson (researcher); Peter Mullings (director); John McGregor (reader); Peter Wheeler (reader); Daphne Oxenford (reader)

What the
papers said

*What the Papers Say – after Panorama the longest-running programme
in the history of British television – was finally killed off in 2008.*
PETER WHEELER, *who worked on the programme for 37 years, writes its obituary*

Sidney Bernstein, who first created Granada in the Fifties, was a great admirer of the circus greats Barnum & Bailey and even had etchings of them on his office walls. Their mantra 'Play it in a Big Top' was a guiding principle for GTV.

Like many of Bernstein's formats in the early days of Granada, *What the Papers Say* was American in origin. 'Papers', 'WTPS' or 'P609' (if you were claiming expenses against its slender budget) was based on the premise that most people only read one newspaper and so absorb only one political interpretation of events. The idea was simple – a fifteen-minute survey of the week's news by a journalist-presenter using autocue, and press cuttings read by a team of actors. There were no visual distractions, making it easy for the viewer to concentrate on the written and simultaneously spoken word.

It was, as one legendary producer, Derek Granger, claimed, 'the fastest ride on the fairground'. A hundred and twenty different shots in twelve minutes were not uncommon. And due to the primitive technology of those days, a single mistake meant going back to the beginning and starting all over again.

Derek Granger came to Granada from the theatre, and later directed Granada's famous adaptation of *Brideshead Revisited* (or *Bridesmaid Redecorated* as it was known in GTV). He worked with great intensity and would frequently use the spectrum to convey his instructions to the readers.

'Page nine is too green,' he would say, or 'Page twelve needs a touch more purple.' My favourite note from Derek, a propos a paragraph from the *Daily Mail*, was 'I want it a little higher ... and ... and as if over sandpaper.'

On one famous occasion Derek was in the production gallery during rehearsal and concluded (wrongly as it happens) that we readers were treating the script with too much frivolity. Clutching the paper tightly in his fist he came down the stairs two at a time, and with flushed face and bulging eyes confronted the team: 'Well if you're remotely interested in my opinion,' he shouted, 'I think the whole show is a fucking Jacobean tragedy of blood!' And with that, he stormed out of the building.

Over the years there was a variety of producers (Brian Armstrong, Michael Ryan, Brian Morris and Brian Blake) and a huge roll call of presenters including Brian Inglis, Bernard Levin, Michael Parkinson, Paul Foot and, later, men like Robert Fox, Max Hastings and John Sweeney. It was the range of styles and the mix of stories that made life so fascinating to the voice-over crew.

We all had our own characters. Daphne Oxenford, who came with a pedigree of comedy gained from working in revue with Joyce Grenfell and a voice forever associated with *Listen with Mother,* was always Osbert Lancaster's famous cartoon creation Maudie Littlehampton. John McGregor, who had understudied Laurence Olivier, brought a Shakespearean dimension to the team, while the late lamented Frank Duncan was capable of giving full weight to, say, the tragic events in Aberfan before moving effortlessly to lighter stories. When increasing deafness forced Frank to retire he left me a note which I still treasure: 'Thank you, not so much for the professionalism at the wicket, which I would have expected, but far more for the companionship in the pavilion.'

What the Papers Say gained a great deal of prestige from its annual awards presentation at the Savoy. The menu traditionally included Lancashire hotpot and a leading politician was invited to present the prizes accompanied by extracts from the work of the winners. For me, it was an occasion fraught with danger. I remember having to quote Jim Callaghan's famous line, 'Crisis, what crisis? I see no crisis', with the man himself standing tight-lipped only three feet away from me.

It was at one of these award lunches that Charles Allen, then Chief Executive of Granada, called the reading team to their feet as representing the 'highest standards of British Broadcasting'. As the applause died away, we sat down and Delia Corrie, another WTPS regular, made the extraordinary remark 'We're all doomed!'

It should have prepared me for a phone call from the executive producer a few months later, when the show was on its summer break. 'Hello, Peter, good news and bad. The good news is that *Papers* returns from its summer break in September. The bad news is that you're all fired.' No reason was given.

When the new team took over, the programme changed a lot. The voices were now recorded separately from the presenter, thus robbing the show of the rapport that had meant so much. Lesser-known journalists replaced their giant predecessors, and the programme (now shown on the BBC) was reduced to ten minutes in length and ended up on BBC2 at teatime on a Saturday.

In its infinite wisdom the BBC has now finally axed *What the Papers Say*, perhaps to make way for another cookery programme or Big Brother's Little Brother's naughty out-takes.

WTPS – RIP.

> ## It was 'the fastest show in the fairground'. A hundred and twenty different shots in twelve minutes were not uncommon – and a single mistake meant going back to the beginning and starting all over again

William Keegan's
FINANCIAL GLOSSARY

Getting to the bottom of impenetrable financial-speak

BANKERS: Gamblers who, when they lose, are bailed out by the state.

OPM: Other People's Money. Much loved by banks, building societies and entrepreneurs. Bill Richards, the chairman of the failed Dome Petroleum Company, once said: 'We weren't really successful in [oil] exploration, but the important thing is that we did it with other people's money.'

LIBOR (The London Interbank Offered Rate): The rate at which banks don't lend to one another *[with thanks to Professor Willem Buiter]*.

CAPITALISM: An economic system which Keynes described as depending on the money-making and money-loving instincts of individuals, and which eventually triumphed over socialism.

SOCIALISM: An economic system which depends heavily on the role of the state and which has recently rescued capitalism.

CREDIT RATING AGENCIES: Highly paid experts who say which countries, banks and corporations are worth lending to and change their minds when the latter collapse.

HEDGE FUNDS: Speculative financial institutions which do not invest in hedges and seldom hedge their bets.

PONZI SCHEME: A pyramid-selling type of 'investment' fund named after an early 20th-century US Italian swindler. Fictional examples of Ponzi include Melmotte in *The Way We Live Now* and Mr Merdle in *Little Dorrit*. Latest example is Mr Madoff who, despite his name, is not fictitious, as his many victims know to their cost (not his).

CREDIT CRUNCH: The sound of bankers grinding their teeth when they refuse to lend to one another, thereby bringing the capitalist system to the brink.

GORDON BROWN: A kind of Messiah who claims to have saved the world by pulling the bankers back from the brink.

LEVERAGE: A smart technical term for debts you can't pay.

'Oh, Jennifer – you and your silly Ouija board'

BANK RATE: The rate at which the Bank of England lends to commercial banks when they won't lend to one another.

NATIONALISATION: A form of public ownership, the commitment to which helped Labour to lose the 1983 election and which saved the world when resuscitated in 2008. (See GORDON BROWN)

'I've spent our way out of trouble!'

SHORT-SELLING: Panic selling by bankers caught with their pants down.

INFLATION: A sustained increase in the average price level which economic policy-makers struggle to avoid.

DEFLATION: A sustained fall in the average price level which causes the economy to seize up and policy-makers to wish they could restore inflation.

QUANTITATIVE EASING: A euphemism for printing money.

BILLION POUND BAIL-OUT: Money which the Government refuses to offer to schools or hospitals but happily gives to banks.

FINANCIAL ENGINEERS: Expensively educated mathematicians who can turn bricks into straw for a large fee.

COLLATERALISED DEBT OBLIGATIONS (CDOs) and STRUCTURED INVESTMENT VEHICLES (SIVs): Inventions by financial engineers that neither they nor their victims understand.

NON-DOMS: Rich foreigners who live in this country but pretend not to for tax purposes.

BARCLAY TWINS: *This entry has been removed on legal advice – Ed.*

DEREGULATION: A relaxation of sensible rules by right-wing governments who affect to believe in the rule of law.

MORAL HAZARD: The belief that banks such as Lehman Brothers should not be bailed out.

DEPRESSION: A feeling of self-pity and *ennui* experienced by financial whiz-kids and entirely unconnected with the ECONOMIC DEPRESSION brought about by the collapse of their financial model.

FINANCIAL MODELS: Beautiful secretaries who lost their jobs when Lehman Brothers collapsed.

ALAN GREENSPAN: A former Master of the Universe who staked his name on deregulation but who has recently owned up.

Former Master of the Universe and Chairman of the Federal Reserve, Alan Greenspan, in 2005

COLLAPSE OF THE FINANCIAL SYSTEM AS WE KNEW IT: What happened when believers in MORAL HAZARD refused to bail out Lehman Brothers.

ECONOMIC DEPRESSION: Something that was never meant to happen but probably will.

SUB-PRIME CRISIS: The collapse of the American housing boom, which Gordon Brown, but few others, blames for the collapse of the Brown boom.

Financial TOP CHUMPS

More priceless contributions to your Top Chump collection! Cut them out and glue them to a piece of card. Swap your Chump cards with your friends.

Get collecting now to be sure of a full set!!

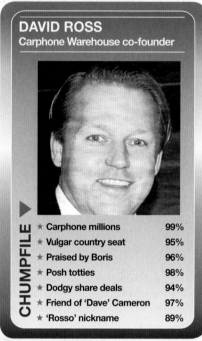

DAVID ROSS
Carphone Warehouse co-founder

CHUMPFILE

★ Carphone millions	99%
★ Vulgar country seat	95%
★ Praised by Boris	96%
★ Posh totties	98%
★ Dodgy share deals	94%
★ Friend of 'Dave' Cameron	97%
★ 'Rosso' nickname	89%

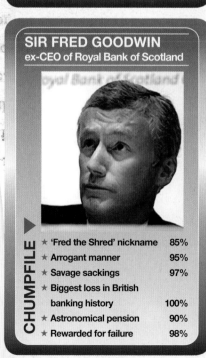

SIR FRED GOODWIN
ex-CEO of Royal Bank of Scotland

CHUMPFILE

★ 'Fred the Shred' nickname	85%
★ Arrogant manner	95%
★ Savage sackings	97%
★ Biggest loss in British banking history	100%
★ Astronomical pension	90%
★ Rewarded for failure	98%

John Updike

1932–2009

DIANA ATHILL remembers the novelist and literary critic who died in January 2009

We published John Updike at André Deutsch for more than thirty years, starting with *Rabbit, Run* which Victor Gollancz lost in a fit of puritanical pomposity, trying to make John delete a sentence which he considered obscene. André was in New York at the time, heard that John wouldn't do it and instantly offered to publish the book uncensored. He then read it during the flight to Boston, so when he met John there he could tell him sincerely that he was mad about the book, and an author-publisher relationship began, so happy that it can be called a friendship.

John was a publisher's perfect author, expecting a good performance but knowing so much about the process that he was never unreasonable, but André valued him so highly for more than that. He loved him because he saw in him something akin to his stubbornly romantic image of 'the English Gentleman'. This may seem odd given how famously John is 'essentially American' as a novelist, but I too felt that his sensibility was in some way European, and not only because of his unfailing courtesy, tolerance and humour, all of which could have been American. Perhaps it was because of how deeply he was rooted – a quality not often obvious in Americans. Nothing would shift his

André Deutsch loved Updike because he saw in him something akin to his stubbornly romantic image of 'the English gentleman'

mother from her family's farm, and although John escaped to wider horizons as soon as he could, he did have a profound understanding of her feelings (witness his lovely novel *Of the Farm*). Once, catching sight of him trudging along a London street (he had brought his family over for a year and I'd found them a house near me), I said to my companion, 'Look – a Dutch farmer!', which was exactly him at that moment. He was a good son, but there was an edginess in his talk about his mother, and I suspected that it came from resentment at having so much of her in himself.

His importance as a writer has been fully acknowledged since his death. What I keep remembering is his niceness as a man. It's really hard for famous people to remain unaffectedly unpretentious, but John always was. I stayed in his house only once, though I visited him from time to time during both his marriages. That stay I remember vividly because of how unlike 'a glimpse of the author at home' it was. It felt simply like 'staying with the Updikes'. At that time he wrote in a room he rented above a shop in the village, and it was as though he kept his persona as a writer shut away there with his typewriter. How he found time to be as much involved in family life and parish affairs as he was (not to mention what he once called his belated wild oats), I can't imagine.

On a later visit to that house, after he and Mary had separated, she and I looked at some photographs of Italy which he had taken on their last holiday there and I was astonished by their quality: if I'd been told some of them were by Cartier Bresson I would not have been surprised. I can still hear Mary's voice – the mixture of grief and pride in it – when my admiration jolted out of her the words, 'He really is an amazing man'. And so, in a way that inspired affection as well as awe, he was.

Below (from l to r): VS Naipaul, John Updike and Laurie Lee with their publisher André Deutsch

'He stole to support a 320-a-day text message habit'

Let sleeping dogs lie...

A rather unexpected discovery on the search for passion

Dogging was not the first thing on the Poetess's mind when she set off for her autumn mini-break this year, but she insisted she was open to new experiences, and it was certainly something new. It all started with her desire to get away, to leave behind the rat race of similes and haikus in an attempt to 'get back to basics'. And it didn't come more basic than a trip to Canvey Island.

Armed with a faded map and a car on its final warning from the AA, she was accompanied by her companion, Friendy. The specifics of their relationship were unknown, but as Friendy was the only person prepared to sit in the passenger seat, it was generally agreed that they were made for each other.

'We should meet the locals,' she told Friendy as they headed off in the wrong gear. 'And get a feel for their world.' Friendy, calmed by Valium bought on the internet and a flask of coffee laced liberally with cheap brandy, nodded vaguely.

The journey started off uneventfully enough, and in only double the time it should have taken, they arrived on the grey shores of the south Essex coast. Save for one café, four youths and a dog on a large-gauge chain, Canvey Island was closed. 'We don't get the tourists anymore,' the café owner sighed. 'Not enough excitement for them.'

The Poetess was surprised. True, there was a down-at-heel feel to the place and the caravan park looked like it had seen better days, but she was captivated by what she saw as its 'rawness'. 'It has untapped passion,' she told the café man as he handed over the special order scampi butty. The café man smiled. 'Well,' he said, 'if it's passion you're after you should try Two Tree Island.'

After consuming their carbohydrate-fuelled lunch – they were on holiday and Friendy had been feeling a little faint – they took his directions and headed off in search of the passionate place. A half-mile causeway leading out over desolate marshland, marked only by clutches of saplings and abandoned beer cans, eventually brought them to the hub of Two Tree Island: a large car park and a slipway leading into sludge-drenched water. It wasn't exactly what she had in mind.

Milling around in the car park were several men dressed in sports jackets and freshly ironed anoraks. 'Excellent,' the Poetess announced. 'Locals. We should

> *Milling around the car park were several men dressed in sports jackets and freshly ironed anoraks. 'Excellent,' the Poetess said. 'Locals. We should meet them'*

meet them.' After draining the contents of her flask, Friendy reluctantly followed.

By the time Friendy caught up, the Poetess was in deep conversation with a man who had introduced himself as Donald, a retired bank employee with a good pension. This latter detail was readily offered. He was more than keen to point out the not particularly obvious appeal of the place.

'Over there are two very good hides,' he explained, pointing towards a couple of almost shattered sheds. 'And you can always get a place in the car park.' The Poetess said that was good to know, but what were the hides for? Donald lent in, conspiratorially. 'The wildlife,' he said, tapping his nose with his forefinger. 'Some of us like to be discreet.' Even by the Poetess's literary standards, this was obscure.

Out of the corner of her eye, the Poetess spotted another man hovering. 'No need to be shy,' she said. 'We're keen to meet the locals.' The man blushed. 'Rough car,' he mumbled. There was no denying it. 'Roomy in the back?' he pressed. 'Yes,' the Poetess replied, truthfully. With that the man shuffled off towards the vehicle. 'What's he doing?' the Poetess asked. 'Getting a good position,' Donald explained. The Poetess and Friendy looked perplexed. 'For your dogging,' he continued. 'But we didn't bring a dog.' The Poetess insisted. 'That's okay,' Donald replied. 'At our age we don't expect anything too fancy.'

Out, out, damn Oz!

While staying as a house guest of **LAURENCE OLIVIER** *and* **VIVIEN LEIGH,**
TRADER FAULKNER *once found himself stuck in the middle of a bizarre argument*

'and he refuses to come down.' Olivier sauntered over, looked up and with a perfect Aussie accent called, 'Hey Mario! I'm Larry, your new boss, and I've got a bloody problem with the show tonight. A quick pow-wow over a beer and together we could crack it.' Mario shot down like a monkey on a greasy pole.

'Oh, Sir Laurence...'

'Call me Larry. Let's go to the pub for a schooner of lager. You're the only man who can sort this out.'

Olivier had his man, and the flying scenery moved up and down like a whore's knickers.

That first night opened on an empty stage. A door opened and a figure like a crippled red and black spider hobbled athletically down to the footlights.

An unmistakeable voice broke the stunned silence. 'Now is the winter of our discontent,' every syllable articulated, virtually spat at his audience. It was the first time Australian audiences had seen Olivier in the flesh.

Later in the play, when we'd all shouted that Richard should be crowned king, he seized a bell-rope and swung himself out over the stalls and back on to the stage. We were watching a consummate actor and showman.

L aurence Olivier would have been 102 years old on May 22nd 2009. I first met him when I was an extra in his *Richard III* at the Tivoli Theatre, Sydney, in 1948. When he arrived in Australia with Vivien Leigh to lead the Old Vic's tour, 'the country had seen nothing like their reception since the visit of the future George VI and Queen Elizabeth in 1926,' as my mother put it.

Six of us had been selected from the cast and were lined up to meet the great man by his stage director, David Kentish. On sauntered the unmistakeable, impeccably dressed Olivier, in a brown herring-bone Savile Row suit, brown shoes

Olivier had been watching us through the hinge crack of the partly-opened door. He ordered me to bed, Vivien ordered me to stay

with gold buckles to match by Lobb, and a grey and yellow striped Old Vic tie made specially for him. We all shook hands and he was gone. Kentish took me aside. 'Do you want to see the Governor in action? We've got a very bolshy fly man here called Mario who refuses to cooperate with "a fucking Pom who thinks he can do his classics in a Variety House".'

Presently Olivier returned. 'Your technical problem for tonight is up that iron circular staircase,' Kentish said,

Seven years later, playing Malcolm to his Macbeth at Stratford, I was guest at the Oliviers' weekend retreat, Notley Abbey at Long Crendon, Bucks. Before breakfast one morning, Vivien Leigh, Alan Webb, Rachel Kempson and I were chatting in the walled garden. Olivier was in his loosely corded dressing-gown, regaling us with a hilarious story of how, as Mr Puff in Sheridan's *The Critic*, he'd nearly been castrated when hoisted up too quickly astride a piece of scenery. In full flight with a captive audience, his dressing-gown flew open. A bee which was hovering about made a beeline for what must have looked like unfamiliar and inviting territory. I wish I'd had a camera: the bee was persistent but Larry was too nimble.

Olivier showed me round the various rooms of Notley Abbey, pointing out what he and Vivien had done to make it theirs. He had landscaped the garden and planted trees along the drive and hedges. Vivien had masterminded the interior decoration. I remember there were three guest bedrooms, one pale green, one pink and one pale blue. Opening the wardrobe in the oak-panelled master bedroom, Olivier revealed a tie rack on which a collection of ties hung. Among them were two identical Old Vic ties, one of which I had seen him wearing at our first meeting on stage at the Sydney Tivoli. I reminded him of this. Impulsively he pulled one out. 'Here, baby!' he said. 'Have one. I don't need two, and when you wear it you'll remember us as we were then.' I wore it for years until it was threadbare. Eventually I threw it out because seeing it reminded me of a man who was impulsively kind but whom success had made both studied and very wary.

He was a benign, avuncular friend until the night Vivien and I drove down to Notley one weekend. (Olivier and a crowd of guests followed soon after.) Sitting alone together over a drink, Vivien asked me about Peter Finch, with whom I had trained and worked in Sydney. They had become lovers on the film *Elephant Walk*

'I had his cremation videoed – so I could watch him burn again and again'

and the affair was still current.

'Oh! Darling Peter is such a wonderful lover. He performs like a naughty but very exciting faun. With Peter, it's *après midi à deux*! In combat would you choose Excalibur or a fish knife? Need I say more?'

I thought, 'Stop! I don't want any part of this.' I was sitting opposite a partly opened door through the hinge crack of which Olivier had been watching us. Vivien was comparing their 'memberships' when he strode in and ordered me to bed. Vivien ordered me to stay.

Desperate to get off the hook, I suggested that as it was a brilliant moonlit night, we three should finish our drinks, take a walk round the garden and then I'd be more than happy to go straight to bed.

'A brilliant diplomatic solution,' said Vivien. Olivier reluctantly agreed, so we walked arm in arm round the abbey and I made my escape.

I must have fallen asleep on my bed fully dressed. At 6 am I woke with a jolt, conscious of a Richard III-like presence hovering too close for comfort.

'Baby, I want you out of the house now,' he spat.

'Now? But it's only six o'clock.'

'After breakfast, fathead. You can say you have to get back to Stratford. I'm going to have Vivien certified.'

Breakfast was a nightmare. Vivien bubbled with excitement. She was planning a picnic at Minster Lovell. I apologised profusely that I had to leave – 'My landlord has arranged a driving lesson.'

'Simply ring and cancel,' Vivien ordered.

'They're not on the phone.'

'Then send him a telegram, for goodness' sake.'

I was out of my depth, and by now I had had Olivier in a big way. He had got me into this mess.

Mercifully, Vivien must have twigged what was afoot – 'Well, of course,' she said, 'if you have to go, you must.'

I went. It was the end of a beautiful friendship. And, of course, Olivier never certified Vivien. After all, they were both due on stage the following day.

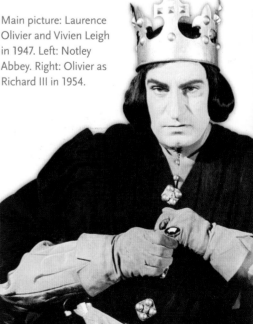

Main picture: Laurence Olivier and Vivien Leigh in 1947. Left: Notley Abbey. Right: Olivier as Richard III in 1954.

Every cloud...

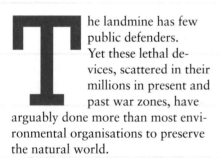

During his travels to international war zones, **Patrick Cockburn** has discovered the one positive consequence of conflict: the local wildlife is thriving

The landmine has few public defenders. Yet these lethal devices, scattered in their millions in present and past war zones, have arguably done more than most environmental organisations to preserve the natural world.

I was recently on the edge of the demilitarised zone (DMZ) which has divided North and South Korea for half a century. From a watchtower on the southern side a wonderful view of the Imjin and Han rivers glittered in the sunlight. In between the heavily fortified front lines, thick scrubland provided a wholly safe sanctuary for wildlife. Nobody could fire a gun without provoking an international incident. A large poster on the southern side warned people against leaving the main road. It depicted a leg with a black boot descending on the prong of an anti-personnel mine, with explosive results. Roads and villas are spreading through the forested hills around the capital Seoul, but so long as Korea remains divided, nothing will be built in the DMZ.

I have always thought war is good for nature. One of the most beautiful places I have ever been in is the Panjshir Valley running along the southern flank of the Hindu Kush mountains north of Kabul in Afghanistan. The long years of fighting destroyed the bridges which have often been rebuilt with great ingenuity out of tree trunks. Nobody has repaired the few roads for decades, so many Afghans ride horses or mules – or walk. There is no electricity because the power plants have been destroyed. Rusting old Soviet tanks

Landmines have arguably done more than most environmental organisations to preserve the natural world

abandoned in the 1980s are used as fencing for fields and look part of the natural order of things. Even where there are no mines or unexploded bombs the violence has been enough to prevent anybody building, so once we had crossed the Hindu Kush we drove along river beds to reach the Amu Darya river (the Oxus) dividing Afghanistan from Tajikistan.

I sometimes feel a little guilty enjoying these unspoilt wildernesses that are protected by war or the threat of war. Wonderful to look at for the passing traveller like myself, but less fun for the permanent inhabitants forced to live without bridges, roads and electricity. At the same time,

it would be good if peace, when it comes, should not lead to the destruction of these extraordinary, if accidental, sanctuaries. It used to be, for instance, that one of the most beautiful parts of Southern Lebanon was the area where Israeli and Hezbollah forces fought for control before the Israeli withdrawal. Elsewhere in Lebanon the smallest bird was in danger from local hunters. But high above the front lines, eagles and kites wheeled in perfect safety – no hunter would go anywhere near the area.

Last year I was in the Kandil mountains in Iraqi Kurdistan along the Iranian border – one of the world's great natural fortresses. Even Saddam Hussein's army could not penetrate here, where the mountains plunge into steep ravines. Herds of cattle with bells around their necks grazed in meadows carpeted with wild flowers. Farmers cut hay with scythes in small fields and built small haycocks. As in Afghanistan, there were no roads. These are unlikely to be built any time soon since the Turkish airforce has started attacking anything that moves along the mountain tracks.

• Patrick Cockburn won the Orwell Prize for journalism in 2009

ILLUSTRATION BY PETER BAILEY

TICKET-RESERVATION

GROUP ADT

Jane's fighting dogs

Humans are not the only objects of photographer **JANE BOWN**'s *observant eye*

'When I move about, I usually see dogs,' says Jane Bown. And she has photographed them wherever she has travelled – sitting among greetings cards (below left), in an antique shop (opposite top) or at the dog show, Crufts (opposite bottom). Closer to home, her own dog Bruin is pictured, left, with her cat, Queenie. Below right: Bruin looks wistfully out of the garden gate.

LIKE YOU, WE COME TO THE DALES FOR A CHANGE. IT IS VERY BEAUTIFUL EVERYWHERE. SWALEDALE AND ARKENGARTHDALE ARE VERY INSPIRING, AND PEACEFUL MOST OF THE TIME.

Not so grim Up North

Life in the Pennines

Illustrated by Peter Brook

It is the extent to which I know this Pennine community and its lore, its past and its present, its anguishes and its rejoicings, the extent to which I am encouraged to share these things, that persuades me most of all that this is, and has been for a quarter of a century, my home in every meaningful sense, though my origins lie a good fifty miles away. I have been admitted to the anecdotes that tell of things only the insiders know, often round my dinner table or theirs.

Old Bob, who was our village sage until he died not far short of his century, was the last old-fashioned blacksmith working in this dale, and he once told me how 'When I were doin' my time,' (serving his apprenticeship before the First World War) 'we used to shoe cows as well as 'osses.' The cattle had been driven on the hoof from Scotland on their way to the English Midlands and even beyond, and by the time they reached the dale they were too footsore to continue unshod.

Next time I was down at the forge, Bob reached up to a shelf beside his anvil and produced two small, shiny and elliptical metal plates, one for each side of a cloven hoof. 'Aye,' he said, 'they reckoned to get t'beasts as far as Smithfield sometimes wi' a pair o' those tacked on.' Nor were cattle the only farmstock tended so carefully. Before the Second World War, most families here kept geese, as Emma still does today; and, as Christmas approached, the whole village flock, dozens of them, would be driven to market seventeen miles down the dale. As they set off, each bird was made to waddle through a trough of tar and then another of sand to protect its feet from the abrasions of the road.

I look out of my study window and watch my neighbours, and I know much more than any outsider could ever know about the jigsaw puzzle of their lives. Nowhere else in the world do I enjoy such intimacy. Nowhere else do I hear all the local gossip. Sometimes I get this intelligence within a few hours: at the very least I hear it over a cup of tea on Friday afternoon when Kath comes to clean. There are other conduits of information whose appetite for gossip is inexhaustible and whose swiftness in transmission is truly spectacular. Say something in confidence to one of these at lunchtime and you can be sure it will be common knowledge by dusk.

And yet such eagerness to breach the individual's privacy is a form of incorporation in itself, placing that person identifiably in the community. Indifference would be much worse to bear, because it would signify a total lack of interest in whether you came or went. That is a very urban, certainly a metropolitan, response: here is its antithesis, not the place to be if your temperament welcomes the anonymity of NW3.

So is something else. If I were to drop dead on the streets of London – or even Manchester or Leeds – the first half dozen people in the immediate vicinity would very probably step over or walk round me, wanting to distance themselves as quickly as possible from an unfortunate incident that could disrupt their day. If I collapse within, say, a mile of this house, the chances are very high that whoever is the first person to come by will say 'Eeee, it's Geoffrey!' They will then do something about it. And that is what real belonging comes down to in the end.

GEOFFREY MOORHOUSE

Modern life

What is...
sledging?

IT USED TO BE another name for tobogganing but sledging has acquired another meaning in modern times, and indeed another season. In cricket, it is the hurling of insults and barbed remarks at the batsman by the fielding side, delivered in a loud voice with the aim of unsettling him to such an extent that he will over-react and be dismissed with a foolish stroke: what the Australians, widely held to be the modern masters of this black art, call 'mental disintegration'. It has become so widespread that India threatened to withdraw from their recent tour of Australia after their off-spinner Harbhajan Singh was accused of insulting Australia's Andrew Symonds, himself no shrinking violet.

Sledging has gone on since cricket was first played. Two notorious practitioners were W G and E M Grace...

Although some think it a modern phenomenon, sledging has gone on since cricket was first played. Two notorious practitioners were the great W G Grace and his older brother E M, known as 'The Coroner', for such was his off-field profession. Fielding close to the wicket for Gloucestershire in the second half of the nineteenth century, the brothers Grace kept up a constant chirping with each other in broad Bristolian about the ability, or lack of it, of the batsman. And, for all its 'Play up! play up! and play the game!' image, as expounded by Sir Henry Newbolt, cricket has always had a tough underbelly, as the Bodyline crisis of 1932–1933 showed.

The *bons mots* of the Yorkshire and England fast bowler Fred Trueman were treasured by players and fans alike, although

Glenn McGrath: 'So what does Brian Lara's d*ck taste like?'; Ramnaresh Sarwan: 'I don't know. Ask your wife.' McGrath: 'If you ever f**king mention my wife again I'll f**king rip your f**king throat out.' Antigua, 2003

many of them were aimed at the umpires and his own team-mates and so do not, strictly speaking, qualify as sledging. The best of them have a wry wit: 'Don't bother, son,' he told a young incoming Australian batsman who was trying to shut the pavilion gate behind him, 'you won't be out there long enough.'

Playing on the old county ground at Hastings (now alas a supermarket, I believe), I was myself sledged by a team-mate, none other than the late Bill 'Bearders' Frindall, the BBC's cricket statistician. We needed quick runs but I was having trouble getting them against a tight attack, so Bill went into the scorebox, which housed the public address system, switched on the microphone and announced to the entire ground: 'Come in number six, your time is up.' I ran myself out shortly afterwards, to everyone's relief.

Sledging really came into its own in Australia in the 1970s. The actual term is said to date from a barbecue attended by several Australian cricketers, one of whom made an inappropriate remark to a woman. He was called to order by John Benaud, brother of the more famous Richie, who told him he was 'as subtle as a sledgehammer'. The offender was instantly nicknamed 'Percy Sledgehammer', and the abbreviated word rapidly came to mean an over-the-top remark on the cricket field.

A lot of the best – or worst – sledging stories therefore tend to involve Australians, but plenty of players can give as good as they get when subjected to what passes for Australian wit. 'How's your wife and my kids?' the Australian wicketkeeper Rod Marsh is reputed to have inquired of Ian Botham as he arrived at the crease to bat. 'She's fine but the kids are retarded,' Botham replied. The exchange gives a good idea of the intellectual level of most such encounters.

As he struggled with the bat against Australia, the England bowler Jimmy Ormond was (reasonably) told by an exasperated Mark Waugh, twin brother of Australia's captain Steve: 'Mate, there's no way you're good enough to play for England.' Ormond shot back, 'Maybe not but at least I'm the best player in my family.'

The best sledge in recent history was delivered by the genial Zimbabwean allrounder (in every sense) Eddo Brandes. Batting against the great Australian fast bowler Glenn McGrath, Brandes kept playing and missing. Eventually, McGrath shouted at him, 'Eddo, why are you so fat?' 'Because, every time I f**k your wife she gives me a biscuit,' replied the unruffled Brandes, reducing the Australian fielders to helpless laughter at their countryman's discomfiture.

ROBERT LOW

'He says I have the reasoning ability of a man twice my age. Isn't that great?'

Ted Heath

The ex-PM behaved like a difficult – but amusing – teenager when he sat for **MARTIN JENNINGS**

I had been commissioned to make a bronze portrait bust of Ted Heath for the Oxford Union and turned up at his house in Salisbury one hot August morning in 1991. I sat and waited in the garden with a coffee. Eventually Heath tacked lugubriously across the lawn and sat down, casting me a long baleful look. He did not appear to be looking forward to the business.

The first thing I needed was a series of photographs of his top half to work from when he wasn't sitting for me. I asked him whether he could put on a suit and tie for the purpose. Releasing a huge sigh of despair he wandered back to the house, appearing what seemed like hours later wearing a jacket and tie but having also put on what must have been the grubbiest pair of sailing trousers in his wardrobe. He was grinning broadly. Clearly it was all going to be a battle of wits.

Modelling of the portrait took place in the large drawing room. Heath was a good hour late for most of the sittings which could be a problem, not least because the morning was the best time to work. Invariably he fell asleep in the afternoon.

As soon as his chin slumped onto his chest I had to down tools. A deep rumbling would emanate from him, the only sound apart from the buzzing of the odd trapped bee in an otherwise deserted house. When eventually I managed to wake him after virtually yelling his name, he would pull his head back and bark at me in turn: 'I wasn't asleep! I was thinking!'

The thinking bit of his face was interesting and I concentrated on it, furrowing the portrait's clay forehead like some of the

'I don't know where babies come from, son. Ask your Google'

Epstein busts I'd been studying. His nose, beloved of caricaturists, was of less interest than the primness of his mouth. Further down, the shelf of his stomach tugged against his jacket in waving sheets. At one point he turned to the sculpture and suggested I treat it to 'a deal less neck'. But how could I? The jowls were the man.

We chatted about this and that. He couldn't understand why the Cathedral choirboys had been allowed home for the summer instead of just being interned for the duration. And he talked about Augustus John, whom he'd met as a younger man. The photo of him with Augustus and his wife Dorelia was the most prominently placed of the host of pictures of himself with world dignitaries that decorated the top of his grand piano. This suggested something about the role of art in his life; I wondered whether one of his gripes with

He suggested I treat it to 'less neck'. But how could I? The jowls were the man

Thatcher was that in his opinion she was just not cultivated enough.

He told me that he was pursuing legislation in Parliament to limit the powers of bogus competition organisers. Some time previously he had received junk mail announcing that he was the lucky winner of a Ford Cortina. He'd had himself chauffeured to the sender's office – a portakabin in some Midlands trading estate. He was filled with glee at the memory of how terrified the manager had looked to find an ex-PM sitting in reception and announcing that he'd come for his Cortina and wanted to drive it home. Not surprisingly the car was unavailable. Heath did however return with a hastily donated crate of cheap champagne in his boot, all of which he poured down the sink.

Heath was provocative, rather like a bored teenager, but there was something very gratifying about his lugubrious wit. Before I drove off with the finished clay he told me in mock despair how feebly the work mirrored its subject. A few weeks later I had a call from his researcher to say that Heath rather liked it and wanted to buy a cast for himself.

ILLUSTRATION BY HEATH

★ Great Bores of Today ★

'... I can't bear the thought of all those ghastly crowds and the waiting in queues and struggling with all those heavy bags so this year Gerald and I are doing all our Christmas shopping online it's so easy you just go to the John Lewis website and it's got everything kitchen equipment duvets menswear carpets and I even got Granny Rose one of those patio heaters and Gerald's ordered a garden furniture set for his brother and Amazon are brilliant for books even if they run out they promise to get it for you of course you may not get it in time for Christmas but at least you don't have to stand behind those awful people in those horrible queues ...'

© **Fant and Dick**

IAN PAISLEY

Mellowed by age – and Mammy

*Oldie of the Year in 2008 and former leader of the Democratic Unionist Party, **IAN PAISLEY** is, at 83, the oldest sitting member of the House of Commons. In 2007 he became the First Minister of the Northern Ireland Assembly, standing down in 2008.*
Interview by **MARY KENNY**

The Rev. Dr Ian Kyle Paisley MP has a reputation for fierceness: he who has denounced the Pope as the Antichrist and launched the famous 'Save Ulster from Sodomy' campaign; he who has said 'No' to so many changes and modernisations that he has been dubbed 'Dr No'; he who has used Biblical language of fire and brimstone against his adversaries since first appearing on the public scene in the 1950s, demonstrating against all moves towards change and reconciliation.

And yet Paisley, in person, seems a cordial old party, throwing his head back as he laughs. The preacher who was once said to affirm the Pauline view that women should keep silent in church, is inseparable from his wife, Eileen, always addressed as 'Mammy', and obediently goes where Mammy leads in the corridors of Westminster. (Eileen is also at Westminster, having been elevated to the Lords as Baroness Paisley in 2006.)

At 83, how does 'Big Ian' look back on his life? Very happily. 'Life is a teaching experience. And sometimes we're amiss in taking the lessons. But the lessons go on.' He feels very well. 'You could reverse my age and make it 28!' He has 'marvellous health,' he says, and 'when the young fellows are exhausted at six o'clock, this old turtle is going on.' Indeed, he'd prefer to be old than young because of the 'teaching experience' of life's reflections.

Paisley was born in Armagh in 1926, the son of an independent Baptist preacher. His mother, a

Shaking hands with his wife Eileen ('Mammy') after winning the election in Ballymena, March 2007

fiery Scot named Isabella, also took to the pulpit and exercised great influence over the family. The Scottish roots remain strong with Ian Paisley to this day: he's friendly with Alex Salmond and feels an affinity with Gordon Brown, the 'son of the manse'.

The culture in which Paisley grew up was austere: no dancing, no liquor and no bobbed hair or lipstick among women, for St Paul disapproved of the shorn head and the painted face. Protestant Ulster was to be defended from both Dublin and Rome: the Vatican was 'the mother of harlots and the abomination of the earth'. Paisley, who preached from the age of sixteen, always used this dramatic language of perfidy with a powerful flourish.

The common view now is that he has mellowed. Does he ever regret using

such pejorative language? He chortles and brushes these points away as mere formulae. These words are 'scriptural terms', he says vaguely, 'but my attitude to individual Roman Catholics has always been respectful.' And it is true that he championed Catholic constituents as energetically as Protestant ones: he once stopped the Department of Transport from running a motorway through the grounds of a convent school.

He also has the politician's reflex of scoring through humour. Latterly, he has been well-received in Dublin, where he is regarded as a bit of a 'turn', especially on TV. Last year, he announced in the Irish capital that he wished he had come to Dublin more often in the course of his life. Pause. 'To evangelise you all!'

And yet Paisley was formerly against every link between Belfast and Dublin. He came to prominence in 1965 when Captain O'Neill, Prime Minister of Northern Ireland, had a much-heralded meeting with Sean Lemass, then Taoiseach. Paisley's protesting banner read: 'No Mass – and no Lemass.' He opposed all liberalisation of the Stormont regime, from the Civil Rights movement to the Sunningdale Agreement of 1973, to the Belfast Agreement of 1998. Would he have done anything differently, looking back? 'I would do a few things differently, yes. But everybody has their own way of doing things. And I lived my life as I believed it.'

Was he too hard on Terence O'Neill? There is no sunny chortle at the mention of the liberalising Unionist. 'Terence

O'Neill was very hard on me. He tried to have me committed to an asylum. He tried to claim that I was mad.' O'Neill was 'not a good man.'

One of Ian Paisley's biographers, Ed Moloney, writes that there are two Paisleys: one is the hell-and-brimstone preacher, but the other is a pragmatic politician who knows when to move in a

equal under the law; if they respect the police' – then he would enter into government with these ex-IRA men. (Irish Nationalists would say that many of the problems arose in Northern Ireland because previously they were not 'equal under the law'.)

'And they have fulfilled their promises. Some not very well. There are some

in the oft-made allegation that he is a man of the 17th century more than the 21st. And yet, he has travelled a road and accomplished something: he certainly will be counted a historic figure.

And he has this benign and optimistic personal side. He gives credit where credit is due – he is pleased and grateful that the Irish Government now honours all Irishmen who fell in the Great War, and he has laid a floral tribute on the grave of John Redmond, the Irish Home Ruler, who died in 1918. Paisley also delights in modern-day Belfast, with all its cheerful improvements, where 'Roman Catholics come up and clap me on the back and say, "We don't approve of everything you say, but we approve of what you have done."'

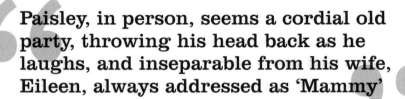

> **Paisley, in person, seems a cordial old party, throwing his head back as he laughs, and inseparable from his wife, Eileen, always addressed as 'Mammy'**

direction that will prove effective. And all his 'Nos' finally came to a 'Yes', when, to the world's astonishment, he went into Government with Sinn Fein, becoming the First Minister in the power-sharing Northern Ireland Assembly, with Martin McGuinness as his Deputy.

A photograph of the pair seen laughing together was widely dubbed the 'Chuckle Brothers' (laughter had erupted when Paisley had said, 'I don't know why people would hate a nice man like me!') He maintains though that the picture is slightly doctored: the two were not sitting side by side at the time the photo was taken. Yet he does not object to the image. 'The picture didn't do me any harm. Better to see that than to come out of these meetings with a long face.' He got along with McGuinness personally. 'Oh yes. We disagreed. We're Ulstermen! There were things we didn't agree on and we left them on the one side and got on with what we could agree on.' Where the former attempts at power-sharing were 'houses built on sand', this one is building on substance.

Why did Dr Paisley – after all his years of opposing dialogue and ecumenism, both political and religious – suddenly perform this volte-face? There is a theory that, after a bout of serious illness, he felt he must move towards peace and reconciliation before meeting his Maker. No, he says, not so. It was simply that Sinn Fein agreed to the three conditions he had always insisted upon: 'If they accept the constitutional position; if they respect the law and that all are

hiccups. But I would not be a Christian if I did not take them at their word.'

There are commentators who ascribe Dr Paisley's more conciliatory development to another factor: Mammy. Eileen Paisley is a quiet but strong-minded wife whose long-term influence is emollient. 'Mammy is the ruler!' he chortles. And Mammy says that Ian has indeed changed for the better over the years.

Not all readers agreed with the Oldie of the Year Award to Dr Paisley. He certainly is a man of paradox, and his opinions have often come across as harsh and unbending. His 'Save Ulster from Sodomy' campaign in the 1970s would today be called homophobic: though he says now that 'we pray for homosexual persons – we do not mock them.' There is some justice

The Paisleys have five children and ten grandchildren, all of them Biblical Christians, and all of them teetotallers for whom liquor remains 'the Devil's buttermilk'. None of their children rebelled against the family values. He was both 'very strict and very liberal' as a parent – his offspring were given boundaries, but told they had to make their own choices. As a grandfather he is 'very indulgent'.

He is tickled that Liam Neeson is to play him in a biopic of his life. But who will play Mammy? For she is perhaps the ultimate shaper of the man.

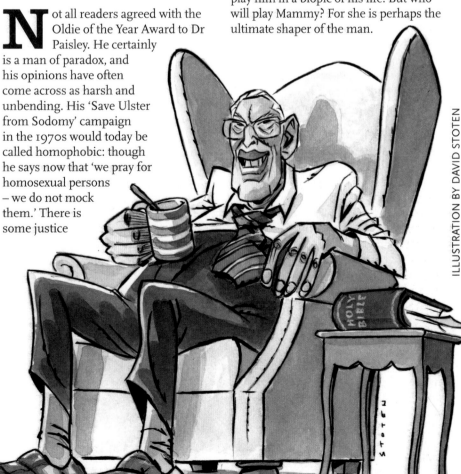

Temples *of* *inconvienience*

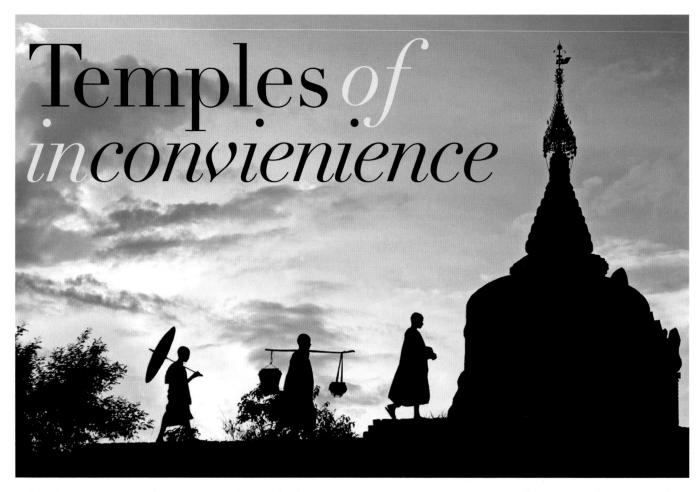

Ah, the serenity, the peace, the enlightenment – **DAVID ERDAL** *desperately wanted to become a Buddhist monk. But a few weeks in a remote temple in the shadow of Mount Fuji saw his meditations take a less spiritual turn...*

The religious gene, if it exists, has always tended to cause havoc in the world. The gene ran strongly through my maternal ancestors. Those affected rarely followed the doctrines of conventional religious institutions, committing themselves instead to profound faith in a variety of equally demented notions. My mother died of breast cancer that she had preferred to treat with white powders and spirit potions rather than conventional medicine. Her father used to converse with fairies in the wild parts of his garden and, inspired by a Russian mystic, spent a fortune funding excavations in Constantinople in search of the Holy Grail. His efforts uncovered the magnificent mosaics of the previously unknown palace of Justinian. He had hoped for much more.

Looking back on my own bumpy life, I have to conclude that I too am a carrier. I was cured of belief in any god at an early age because the official representative of religion at my prep school, the deputy headmaster, was a sadist. But in my 1960s teenage years the gene had me primed for conviction. The trigger turned out to be Alan Watts's book *The Way of Zen*, soon reinforced by Philip Kapleau's autobiographical account of achieving enlightenment, *The Three Pillars of Zen.*

The attractions of Zen were multiple. First, there was no crazed, demanding, supervisory god. Second, Zen seemed to be gloriously empirical: the important thing was to sit and meditate and see what happened, not to recite or discuss doctrines. Third, there was a robust iconoclasm, a determination to avoid what they called 'stinking of religion'. This produced sayings like: 'If you meet the Buddha, kill the Buddha!' Finally, there was a freshness about most of the teaching texts. They had few traces of doctrinal prescription, consisting largely of questions asked over the centuries by monks living a life of meditation, and the answers given at the time by the head monks in their monasteries. One example that particularly struck me was:

Japanese monasteries were tough in the 1960s. The one I ended up in was a spectacularly beautiful 300-year-old temple

Question: 'What is Buddha?' (This means: 'What is the ultimate reality?' It is not a question about the historical person but about what he discovered through meditation.) The answer this time was:

'The stick that you use to scrape the shit off your bum.' There was no toilet paper in medieval Japanese monasteries.

All this was rather refreshing. The answer was not in any book. Enlightenment could be recognised not by any creed but by changed behaviour, exhibiting tenderness, compassion, generosity.

Fascinated by the idea of attaining the freedom and generosity of enlightenment, I resolved to travel to Japan to become a monk. For life. (The gene rarely allows half measures.) So in 1968, when my fellow-students were dividing their time between pop concerts and riots, I set off on the Trans-Siberian railway to join a Japanese monastery for the rest of my life.

We are told that when the Buddha was nearing enlightenment his last temptation was posed by a beautiful woman. For me, temptation took the form of a gorgeous Mongolian girl who filled the samovars and kept the carriages clean on our four-day journey through Siberia. She made it clear that she would love to have an affair with a 'gentleman' like me. To my great regret, looking back, I turned her down, afraid of KGB entrapment. Why the KGB might have wanted to divert me from spending my life in a monastery I have no idea. But it was terror, not virtue, that kept me virtuous.

Japanese monasteries were tough in the 1960s, and probably still are. The one I ended up in was a spectacularly beautiful 300-year-old wooden temple in a forest near Mount Fuji. It had a soaring roof supported by four huge polished tree trunks over a suspended wooden platform where we meditated and chanted daily. We slept in rows on tatami mats, rose at 5 am, slid back the paper walls to open up the forest all round and chanted till 6.30 am. As dawn broke the frogs would join in from the pond along two sides of the building. It was exhilarating, exotic, exciting.

Most of the time was spent in meditation. Even when we were doing the daily chores – cleaning the buildings, weeding the paths, digging in the fields – there was no chatting. For my meditation the head monk set me the task of solving a centuries-old puzzle. A monk asked his teacher, 'Has that dog got the Buddha nature?' The teacher barked, 'Mu!' The literal translation of 'mu' is 'it does not have'. But there are many texts to tell you that everything has the Buddha nature – that is, everything is included in ultimate reality. So the teacher had said

The process of meditation itself was unexpected. Far from producing the hoped-for serenity, it plunged me into chaotic reflections

'no', contradicting the teaching. You soon realise that there is little point in thinking about it; you just settle down to meditate.

The process of meditation itself was unexpected. Far from producing the hoped-for serenity and enlightenment, it plunged me into chaotic reflections of real life. And there was no way out.

For example, instead of rising above distractions to float serenely above it all, I was possessed by sexual fantasies. The Mongolian girl proved an extraordinary lover. I lost whole hours in erotic daydreams. This was stimulating, but it was clearly not enlightenment.

Behind these fantasies came other, less enticing pictures and feelings. Past humiliations smarted anew, and there was an abundance of anger – anger at things that had been done to me at

BILL PROUD

boarding school by a big boy in the rhododendron bushes, and at unjust beatings by authority figures. It was not all inward-looking – rage and sorrow mingled over what the Americans were doing to the Vietnamese and to their own young soldiers.

While this occupied my head and heart, my body was living the monastic life. Unfortunately for Westerners, Japanese monks live on the floor. I had a stiff knee from a recent operation, but had to sit cross-legged and motionless for long periods in meditation and kneel for many other activities. Eventually my knee gave up the struggle and ballooned.

I hobbled in to see the head man and asked to be allowed to sit on a stool.

He laughed and rang the bell, signifying 'end of interview'. That evening I gathered my things and crept out, my lifetime commitment at an end after two months.

Money soon ran out and I spent a couple of nights sleeping on the steps of Yokohama tube station. It was December, piercingly cold. Desperate for warmth, I accepted a Japanese man's offer of a bed for the night. He turned out to have a similar plan to that of the boy in the rhododendron bushes. This time, however, I could just walk away. I left the boarding house where he had taken me and found myself in the red-light district of Yokohama.

The rest of the night passed trudging the streets to keep warm, and at last a sort of serenity opened up, just walking on, letting everything be, including me.

Towards dawn a youth manning a food stall and wanting to practise his English gave me a portion of squid stew. It lives still in my mind, nearly forty years on, as probably the best food I have ever had.

'Somebody told her she looked good in a soft light'

Positano

Overpriced, overcrowded, and with a beach like a toilet, the jewel of the Amalfi coast fails to work its legendary magic on **CLARE CLARK**

John Steinbeck has a great deal to answer for, not least the assertion that he got through up to sixty pencils a day (did he smoke them?) His worst crime, however, was writing a love letter to Positano in 1953 which he concluded thus: 'Nearly always when you find a place as beautiful as Positano, your impulse is to conceal it. You think, "If I tell, it will be crowded with tourists and they will ruin it, turn it into a honky-tonk and then the local people will get touristy and there's your lovely place gone to hell."'

Congratulations, John. Before I went to Positano I had a wonderful image of a heartbreakingly picturesque fishing village built into vertiginous cliffs above a turquoise sea, a heavenly spot where women who contrived to make Capri pants and silk headscarves look elegant skipped gracefully up and down steep stone paths. Positano would seduce me, everyone said. Despite the expensive boutiques and restaurants and the angina-inducing hotel bills, nothing could rob the place of its magical allure.

They lied. Positano is, quite simply, horrible. It is not the time we spent getting there that I hold against it, twenty miles that took two hours of crawling hell on cliff roads barely wide enough to accommodate a bicycle. It was the time it took to get out again, besieged, furious and weeping blood from both our ears and our wallets.

We stayed in one of the town's most famous hotels, Le Sirenuse. Our room cost just shy of 1,000 euros per night and was the size of a slightly inadequate cupboard. When we escaped to the pool we found a sunbathing area so tiny that the sun-loungers touched edges. We were told we were lucky to find one free – usually you had to be at the pool by 9 am to ensure you got one. Well, fair enough,

Our room cost just shy of 1,000 euros per night and was the size of a slightly inadequate cupboard

I say. What do you expect for 1,000 euros a night? I lay down next to an obese American banker whose flesh overflowed onto my towel. For an hour without pause, he shouted angry instructions into his cell phone. In the pool itself, the size of a kitchen sink, more Americans shouted at each other in voices that would have carried far enough to have allowed their neighbours in Texas to join in.

Shaken, we headed for the beach. Everywhere on the walk down we were bombarded by hawkers selling nasty bikinis and even nastier jewellery. Red-faced tourists in elasticated slacks jostled together, swearing as they bumped their wheeled suitcases down the cobbled steps. Outside every restaurant there was a man posted to bark at you as you passed or even catch your arm so that he might give you the hard sell. There was nowhere that was not packed with people, heaving with noise and the pervading odour of sweat and discontent.

The beach, when we reached it, was just as overcrowded, the loungers set almost as close together as the ones at the hotel. The sand was a delectable dirt brown. We headed for the sea, intent upon a cooling swim. At the water's edge the receding tide had arranged a charming collage of bottles, wrappers and used tampons. I dipped a tentative foot into the water and found my ankle nudged by several discarded Band-Aids.

We stayed for three days. I would have had a more relaxing holiday if I'd pitched a tent in Oxford Street at the start of the summer sales. I blame John Steinbeck. He would have been better off smoking those pencils after all.

Virginia Ironside

Those snookey-okum back-stabbing bickerers make me glad to be single

I had a small party recently, and as she said goodbye, a friend added: 'I so enjoyed myself. It was such a success. And do you know why? There were no couples.'

She was right. There were a couple of gay couples, and a couple of people who'd only just started living together, but there were no actual couply couples, people who have grown into each other like ivy into a tree.

I hasten to add that many of my best friends are couples who've grown into each other like ivy into a tree. And there is something very comforting about being with them. I always feel, even if they're younger than me, that I'm back to being a child again, but this time with very nice and attentive parents indeed. It's those terrible old bickering couples that I can't stand. The ones who call each other darling all the time. 'I think you're wrong, darling,' says one to the other. 'It was Wednesday.' 'No, love of my life, it's you who've got it wrong. It was Thursday.' 'I hate to contradict, sweetie,' replies the other, 'but you're getting a teensy weensy bit muddly-upply in your oldie agie. I know it was Wednesday.' 'Don't you muddly-upply oldie agie me, light of my life,' replies the other, getting really edgy. 'I have my diary to prove it.' And then, through gritted teeth, 'My angel.' (It's at that point I feel like screaming: 'For fuck's sake, who cares if it was Wednesday or Thursday! Just shut up and get on with it!') They're the ones who, when one tells a story, make frequent corrections to the other's flow. Or, at the very end of some long saga, when they've been interrupted a dozen times, sigh:

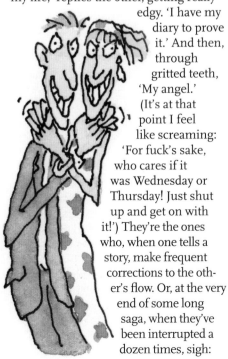

'Sweetie, you're getting a teensy weensy bit muddly-upply in your oldie agie...'

'Who's telling this story, you or me?'

It's at times like those that I thank God that, despite huge bouts of loneliness over the years, I am single.

Another death. This time the untimely demise of my cousin Nigel Acheson, the man who started Loftus Productions, whose programmes are never off Radio Four. But another death means another undertaker. And what a funny bunch they are.

The last undertaker I had dealings with appeared when my father died. When speaking to my stepmother, he kept referring to my father as 'hubby' and it took a while for us to catch on to what he meant. And when we revealed that, apart from designing the backs of the decimal coins, my father had done some glass engraving, he replied: 'Grave-englassing. How interesting.'

This one, dressed in a waistcoat, tie and black suit, found it hard even to smile. I wonder if they have been trained to keep a poker face? I imagine undertaker training classes in which they are tickled and barraged with jokes, and the first one to smile is kicked off the course. The moment we were in his room it was like being transported into another age, apart from a bizarre bright metal coffin in the window ('There's a sprung mattress inside'). No computers – everything was laboriously handwritten. Words like 'catafalque' and 'committal' were used, and I remembered a time when I'd been asked to write a client brochure for a large American funeral company, called 'How to Arrange a Funeral'. There were only two problems. They didn't want the word 'body' to be used. They preferred 'the deceased'. And they recoiled at the mention of 'ashes'. What word should I use instead, I asked, baffled. 'Cremains,' they said. At that point I *did* put my foot down.

Leafing through a brochure called 'Reflections', I saw that we could order a coffin with a photograph printed on the side – a country scene, golfing paraphernalia, a rocket, or even – really creepy – one that was painted entirely as the Union Jack. Apart from a vaguely heathery one with a picture of the Highlands, there didn't seem to be one appropriate for the chattering classes. The problem is that it's only after you've signed and sealed the whole ludicrously expensive package – around £2,000, inclusive of limousine – that you remember about the Natural Death Centre who'll organise a woodland funeral in a biodegradable coffin. 'Next time,' I said to myself, rather ghoulishly.

*When **JERUSHA MCCORMACK'S** husband died suddenly, she found the traditional platitudes about grieving to be useless – until she was shown a ball in a jar...*

Enduring Grief

Ten years ago my husband died, suddenly, without warning, after a complicated, if routine, operation. That day a world opened which I had never imagined before.

In the world of the day before, we were safe. My husband was reasonably well. The boys, eleven and seventeen, were growing up fine. We had two secure, professional jobs. Our mortgage was under control. Our anxieties – centred upon ageing parents, the boys at school or office politics – now seem so predictable.

From the moment the hospital rang asking me urgently to come in, I knew my husband was dead. But at the same time I did not know what was going to happen from moment to moment. I did not know what to do.

Yet I knew certain things had to be done in a certain order, even though they were contradictory. I had to go in to the hospital to be told my husband had died, although every instinct told me he was dead. I had to see him to say goodbye, even though I knew he had left. Somehow I had to involve the boys in this, but at the same time I had to protect them.

I remember looking over at them as I put the phone down, thinking: 'I don't have to tell them this. I can just pretend nothing has happened.' Because once I told them, their childhood would be

over. It was then that I made a resolution: however bad this would be, we were going to meet it head-on. That meant, first of all, not being afraid. It was as if I understood, instinctively, that my worst enemy would not be pain, but fear.

Still, when the shock wore off, the pain was intense; so bad at times I could not even find a physical position that was comfortable – much less eat or sleep. But I learned to say to myself, it is only pain. It is not good or bad, but a sign we have been wounded. If we pay attention to the wound, if we do not ignore it, we will heal. But how? Some months before, a Buddhist friend had told me, 'Life is suffering'. Now his words came back, along

with their corollary: 'Everything changes. And everything is interconnected.' Over the first weeks, this became my mantra, my first clue to the way ahead. If everything changes, death is just another change among many. We have been changed and will in turn be changed by what we change.

But the world did not want to accept change. Something had gone missing. So it should be replaced – immediately – to get back to where we were before. Thus, within the year, people started to ask, 'Have you recovered yet?' Recovered what? I would ask myself. My world had disappeared with my husband. I had not only lost a husband and a father to our children, but also income and status. Invitations had started to dry up. The phone calls fell off. My husband's friends, with notable exceptions, avoided me. Evidently, I was a social embarrassment, a wet blanket, the *momento mori* at the birthday party.

Then someone was sure to ask me whether I had begun dating again. What? How do you begin dating when you haven't dated for over thirty years? When you are trying to hold down a full-time job, raise two now vulnerable boys and hold on to your sanity when almost everyone else seems to think you have become another person? All this too on little sleep, poor appetite and scattered concentration. For my mind was no longer my own. It was entirely preoccupied by the question: what do I do now? As I am clearly not going to recover – in the sense that things are never going to be the same again – what direction is open to me? Why, when everyone at some time or another is going to go through this experience, has someone not plotted out some routes for the journey?

Instead of routes, what society offered me were deflections: a whole catechism of clichés as threadbare as they were useless. It was a conspiracy: I would act the poor, mousey, perhaps pious, widow and allow them to inflict these aphorisms on me in the interests of my well-being.

Then someone told me there was a map; it was a book called *On Death and Dying* by Elisabeth Kübler-Ross. She told me I would go through different emotional reactions in a predictable order, beginning with denial and ending with acceptance: 'the five stages of grief.' Very tidy. Now I could get on with it – suffering by schedule.

'Pay attention or I'll sack the lot of you'

Except that when I tried to pay attention to them, the stages got all mixed up – if I could identify them at all. As far as I could see, denial would veer suddenly into acceptance and then back again into anger. I dared not believe in hope.

Then one day I saw a notice for a talk on helping children through bereavement by Barbara Monroe, the Chief

I understood instinctively that my worst enemy would not be pain, but fear

Executive of St Christopher's Hospice in London. When I arrived, what I saw resembled a physics lesson. On the table before her was a very large glass jar. Beside were three balls: one large, one medium-sized, one small. Without a word, she began to stuff the large ball into the jar. With a great deal of effort, she wedged it in.

'There!' she said. 'That's how grieving feels at first. If grief is the ball and the jar is your world, you can see how the grief fills everything. There is no air to breathe, no space to move around. Every thought,

every action reminds you of your loss.'

Then she pulled the large ball out of the jar and put in the medium-sized ball. She held it up again, tipping it so the ball rolled around a bit. 'Maybe you think that's how it will feel after a time – say, after the first year. Grieving will no longer fill every bit of space in your life.' Then she rolled the ball out and plopped in the small ball.

'Now, say, by the second or third year, that's how grieving is supposed to feel. Like the ball, it has shrunk. So now you can think of grief as taking up a very small part of your world – it could almost be ignored if you wish to ignore it.'

For a moment, considering my own crammed jar, I thought of leaving. 'That's what everyone thinks grieving is like,' the voice continued. 'And it's all rubbish.'

I settled back into my seat. Two other glass jars were produced from under the table: one larger, one very large.

'Now,' she said, imperiously. 'Regard.' Silently, she took the largest ball and squeezed it slowly into the least of the three jars. It would barely fit.

Then she pulled the ball out and placed it in the next-larger jar. There was room for it to roll around. Finally, she took it out and dropped it into the largest glass jar. 'There,' she said, in triumph. 'That's what grieving is really like. If your grieving is the ball, like the ball here it doesn't get any bigger or any smaller. It is always the same. But the jar is bigger. If your world is this glass jar, your task is to make your world bigger.'

'You see,' she continued, 'no one wants their grief to shrink. It is all they have left of the person who died. But if your world gets larger, then you can keep your grief as it is but work around it.'

Then she turned to us. 'Older people coping with grief often try to keep their world the same. It is a mistake. If I have one thing to say to all of you it is this: make your world larger. Then there will be room in it for your grieving, but your grieving will not take up all the room. This way you can find space to make a new life for yourselves.'

'This is it!' I said. 'A way out – a way to remake my life.'

That was eight years ago. For what the balls and jars gave was a new way to imagine grieving – and how it might be turned around. Having emigrated in my head to a place where I am neither married nor unmarried, neither desolate nor jubilant, I am now, literally, in a new country – China – and enlarging my life.

'Oh, come on, all I did was forget the milk. I don't need a flippin' lecture!'

Named after Charles-Geneviève d'Eon de Beaumont, a rosy-complexioned courtier at Louis XV's court, The Beaumont Society (TBS) for the discreet transvestite opened in 1966, when a man dressed as a woman could get arrested for disturbing the peace or importuning. It is now the UK's oldest transvestite club and even has a wives' wing for married members.

Tucked away amid the scarred streets of King's Cross, TBS is once again hosting a monthly meeting. As swarms of rocker stalwarts and leather-faced queens flood the area's various drinking holes for another boozy night, a trickle of transvestites gather for traditional tea, sympathy and dress changes. A shy, plumpish man resembling a bank manager arrives in pink shirt and jeans and disappears into the back, returning in a denim skirt and funky T-shirt. A balding transvestite comes dressed in pearls and flowered frock. Fluttering false eyelashes, the bank manager settles in nicely with a biscuit. It is his second time at TBS and he is aglow with happiness.

TBS's chairlady, 'Helen', has long hennaed hair and is dressed in a T-shirt and a sensible below-the-knee skirt. In a soft baritone she advises first-timers where to find the changing-rooms. Just below her Adam's apple dangles a silver butterfly pendant – the trademark of the club.

A robust-looking matron whom I mistake for a member's wife settles in to observe the tiny crowd. Pippa, at sixty-plus, has a grey Diana hairdo and spectacles. Her breasts are suitably full

Trannies and Tea

DAEMIENNE SHEEHAN *talks to members of The Beaumont Society, a pioneering organisation which provides a space in which transvestites can express themselves*

ABOVE: Helen, The Beaumont Society's 'chairlady'

for a nearly six-foot-tall 14-stone woman – and although her skirt, provided by her staunchly Catholic wife, has a dashing beaded edge, she looks like an English matriarch who knows her roses.

Before she told her neighbours about her true wardrobe, Pippa often found herself in the garden, terrified that she had forgotten to remove her nail varnish when one of them wandered over for a chat. 'Recently, I told everyone and I now go to the front door in a dress – bliss!' Pippa reveals that TBS has changed since she joined in the 1970s. 'Take Grayson Perry. I hated him at first. I thought he was making us all look silly. He wanted to come on a Beaumont weekend but was refused because we have a dress code – no fetish, no rubber, nothing funny. But recently, he wrote an article for the TBS magazine.'

Pippa says that many transvestites hope that marriage will distract them from dresses. 'But the urge never disappears. The problem, if you're married, is where do you hide the clothes? Earrings are dangerous – they're so comfortable you forget they're there when you hear the car pull into the drive.'

TBS was Pippa's first 'trannie' home. 'We all have theories why we're trannies and they're probably wrong. I think my mother made me one. When father abandoned us she really struggled, but always made fantastic dresses for my sisters and put all her love into them. She was not demonstrative otherwise, and she hated making boys' clothes. I wanted her love through dresses ... I hate beards,' she adds, 'because I associate them with homelessness. When my father, a drunk, kicked us out, my first beard had started to grow. I don't like men much.'

For many people TBS is 'like having a childhood,' Pippa theorises. 'I expect that's why people eventually leave – they grow up.' She remains loyal to Beaumont but isn't a fan of events like Wedding Dress Day. 'I don't wear wedding dresses,' she says. 'I always go about as a prim old lady doing things that prim old ladies enjoy – visiting galleries and shopping.'

Lynn, an unmarried elderly transvestite, explains: 'I wanted to dress as a girl because I was jealous of the extra attention they got when they dressed up. But because transvestites only dress up occasionally, they go overboard and end up wearing everything. Real women go through the silly dress stages when they're young and learn what suits them. It takes us a lot longer.'

Lynn, who was a child extra in *The World of Suzy Wong*, looks like an elderly Japanese hostess, moving in the same fastidious way. It is only when she speaks, in a surprisingly deep voice for such a small man, that she stands out. As a pensioner, she thinks TBS should offer discount rates for the unemployed and pensioners to increase membership.

'Last night I visited a straight karaoke bar but I'm terrified of discovery,' she reveals. 'It's a series of steps. First you dress up at night because it's easier, then you dress as a woman in the day. Next you speak to someone but your voice is male. The final step is sex.'

Despite retaining regulars like Pippa and Lynn, these are hard times for the elderly stateswomen of the transvestite set. While the median age of TBS members remains fifty-plus, numbers have gone down from over 2,000 in its heyday and from 500 to 400 in the last year. Helen fears that the club's twinset and pearls image, while reassuring for first-timers, is sounding the death knell as a new generation of transvestites opts for the outré hedonistic whirl of rival groups like the Way Out Club. 'The latest generation are into clubbing and being excessive,' Helen admits. 'We offer Beaumont weekends away to places like Hastings and costume museums and have events like Sari Night. Plus we encourage wives to join in.' Helen, who first approached her transvestite self by wearing kilts, says, 'The Way Out Club doesn't appeal to me. They can wear rubber – it's a very different approach.' It is a common TBS refrain.

A flip through their quarterly magazine reveals the genteel world of the TBS transvestite. Stout, comfy-looking men,

Helen fears that the club's twinset and pearls image is sounding the death knell as a new generation of transvestites opt for the outré hedonistic whirl of rival groups

in Marks & Sparks dresses pose amiably in the Dales or share a smile over a cream tea. 'TBS gives people the wings to be what they want, but then they often fly away,' Helen says with a wistful air. 'I suppose we should be glad they've gone out into the wider world but it would be nice if they came back occasionally to say hello. It's a mark of civilisation that groups like ours are allowed to express themselves. But perhaps TBS was needed in less tolerant times and tolerance will be our undoing.' But surely there are still enough shy men out there who want to wear a dress and don't have the nerve? Helen agrees, 'but we have to figure out how to reach them.'

An evening of civilised kindly meetings is drawing to a close. Helen wends her way through the group, calling out 'It's pumpkin time', signalling that those who came as men need to change back. Out in the rubbish-strewn street, the bank manager wonders whether he did his make-up correctly but cannot stop smiling. As he sails off into the rush of a King's Cross night, manoeuvring insouciantly through throngs of glassy-eyed drinkers, he is dreaming of his time with those tender men in dresses. But who knows how long the grand old lady can welcome such courtiers into her parlour?

'He died doing what he loved most – shooting it out with the cops'

Works from the Lehman collection

A rare opportunity for collectors with Christmas in mind

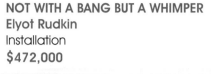
NOT WITH A BANG BUT A WHIMPER
Elyot Rudkin
Installation
$472,000

GENOCIDE 937
Paolo Angelotti
Sculpture, polytungsten substitute
$803,000

SPIRIT OF ST LOUIS
Marlon Kissinger
Limited edition Lithograph
$64,000

WE ARE ALL GUILTY
Amy Minim
Installation
$906,000

The Red Rectangle Private Collection Gallery
645E Sweetbread Lane, adjacent to Hoxton Square,
Hackney, London N1

telephone: 01234 56789
email: buy@redrectanglegallery.com
web: www.redrectanglegallery.com

*'Bryan Steinway's Red Rectangle Gallery, an oasis in the desert
of Hoxton, has taken cutting edge into a new dimension'*

WEEKEND GUARDIAN

THE **BOUNCER'S** TALE

PHIL WARK *can deal with cat-fights and bruisers. But how does he cope when grannies grab his crotch?*

Here I am then, the oldest bouncer in town. Pushing fifty and with a face that could scuttle a thousand ships, I had never realised that my pug ugliness could be an occupational advantage. The job advert didn't specify that an oft broken nose was a requisite but I'm sure it helped with my application.

No chavs, no baseball caps, no drunks, explains my colleague on my arrival at my first job. But this is a popular chain of wine bars on a Saturday night. Are we to turn everyone away? What do I know? Twenty-odd years as a milkman may have tutored me in the art of resisting the entreaties of lonely housewives but it hardly makes me an expert in controlling the masses on a Saturday night, so I keep my counsel. New job; keep one's mouth shut. I'd already blotted my copybook by turning up in a white shirt. Didn't they tell you? It's a black shirt here. Why? I ask. It transpires

that if you wear white shirts you have to chuck them away when you get blood on them. Black shirts don't show the stains. I suppose it makes sense.

The customers begin to arrive. Due to a recent clampdown by the local authority on under-age drinking we have to ask for ID from the more youthful entrants. The first lady to whom I make the appropriate request shows her driving licence. She's 32. Perhaps I am

It's only when we get out into the street that he hits me on the head with a bottle...

too old for this. At least she's flattered. I even get a kiss and I don't get many of those these days. Another lady says that she hasn't got ID but can show me her stretch marks. I decline her kind offer and let her in.

The first fight of the evening erupts. Two young girls are lying on the dance floor pulling each other's hair and

breaking their nails on the other's face. My colleague and I take one each (by which I mean that we separate them) and escort them to the fire exit. We ask them if there is a problem. After a frank exchange of some choice Anglo-Saxon words it becomes manifest that it would be better if they left. I imagine they will continue their pugilistic endeavours elsewhere.

It is one of my tasks to check the toilets every thirty minutes. In the gents I hear an unholy row coming from one of the stalls. The cubicle is shaking amidst loud groans. From the sound of it, they are rutting like boars. I bang on the door. Silence. 'Open the door,' I say. As it swings inwards a face appears. I push in and find another male pulling up his trousers. We're in a town in the South West but it seems appropriate to use my best *EastEnders* accent. 'You two, out now,' I say. They leave, somewhat shame-faced, tails between their legs – for now.

I notice a young man trying to buy drinks at the bar. He is already extremely drunk. 'You've had enough, mate,' I tell him. When I say that we persuade him to leave the establishment, you will understand that although we are not the law, it pays to use the careful language of PC Plod. It's only when we get out into the street that he hits me on the head with a bottle. Fortunately he doesn't hit me hard enough to break either the glass or my thick skull. I relieve him of the bottle and advise his friends to get him home. The matter is 'resolved', as we like to say.

If you work the door properly you can minimise the fights and the couplings, and on some nights nothing happens at all. That's when I wonder if I'd be better off at home watching television. I've got some very comfy slippers. But then the cultural desert that is terrestrial television on a Saturday night is even more barren than a provincial wine bar. Ant and Dec's *Saturday Night Takeaway*? I may be about as hard as Homer Simpson but at least I'm getting paid for working this door.

People ask me if I get scared. The honest answer is only when the grannies attack. For some reason the women who make a beeline for me usually have sticks, which are no impediment to their agility, and I admire their spirit if not their originality. When they try to grasp my crotch (yes, really) they always say the same thing: 'Can you handle me?' I can't help thinking that if I treated them the same way I'd be locked up for sexual harassment.

Change your life.
Do nothing

DO
NOTHING
TO CHANGE
YOUR LIFE

Far from the madding crowd: **STEPHEN COTTRELL,** *the Bishop of Reading, discovered a new philosophy for life while taking a school assembly*

A couple of years ago I was due to lead an assembly at a Church of England comprehensive school that I visited regularly. This is a tough gig: seven or eight hundred adolescents, crowded into a hall first thing on a Monday morning and forced to endure a hymn, a prayer, a worthy talk and, usually, a ticking off. On this occasion my anxiety levels were particularly high since I had not really prepared anything much to say. It was the beginning of Lent and I had a vague idea about encouraging them to take something up rather than give something up, but as I walked to the school I became all too aware that my situation was similar to driving in the fast lane of the motorway with no petrol in the tank and realising you've just gone past the services.

But these moments of panic can also be moments of prayer, moments when we are more open to the wiles of God. And it was almost as I got up to speak that a crazy idea was suddenly born within me. I stood up and found myself saying something like this:

'We live in a crazy, frantic world. Our world is full of movement and noise. Even this morning, in the few hours since you woke up, you have probably filled your time with the radio, the TV, the computer, the PlayStation; you've probably phoned someone and texted half a dozen others. As you got dressed, washed, showered, ate your breakfast and came to school, noise and busyness have accompanied your every move. I believe many of the world's problems are caused by our inability to sit still and

to be quiet and to reflect. I believe that, in this season of Lent, we should try to give up being so frantic, and we should take on some moments of stillness.'

Then I stopped, as if I had lost my thread (actually, it felt as if the thread were being handed to me inch by inch, and even I was not aware what was at the end). And I said to them, 'Hey, you don't know what on earth I'm talking about, so let me give

For a minute I sat still. I didn't say anything and I didn't do anything

'I'm not sure if he's a born again Christian or a smack head'

you a demonstration. Let me show you what I mean. This is what I'm suggesting you do, each day in Lent, for exactly one minute. It will change your life.'

I then picked up a chair, placed it in the centre of the stage, and slowly and carefully sat down upon it, with my feet slightly apart and with my back straight and with my hands resting gently on my knees. And, for a minute, I sat still. I didn't say anything and I didn't do anything. I wasn't even consciously praying. I was just sitting there. And I breathed deeply, and I thought about my breathing. And when I reckoned the minute was over, I stood up.

But before I could say my next bit, there was a huge, spontaneous round of applause. Now, I had done lots of assemblies in that school. On many occasions I had slaved over what I would do or say to capture the imaginations of young people. But I had never had a response like this. In fact, in the days that followed, I was stopped in the street on several occasions by parents who told me that their child had come home and told them about the priest who took assembly and just sat on the stage in silence for a minute and then suggested they might do the same thing. Because, when the applause died down, that's what I'd said. I just suggested that sitting still, being silently attentive to things deep within ourselves and things beyond ourselves, would make a difference. You didn't need to call it prayer. You didn't need to call it anything, because it would be in these moments of sedulous stillness that God could be discovered.

An Orthodox Voice
UFOs and what they do to you

AT ONE TIME, around 1968, I used to see UFOs quite regularly. Mostly they appeared as points of lights darting around in the night sky, more like little fishes than anything technological. Once, encamped with the horse-drawn traveller Mark Palmer and his colourful followers, we saw a luminous, cigar-shaped 'mother ship' over Wells Cathedral, with little lights going in and out of it. Wells choir-boys saw the same thing and it was reported in the local paper. Later, in Scotland, similar lights appeared to a group of us at a bonfire. The locals there were dismissive. That's nothing, we see them all the time, they said. My last sighting, a few years ago, was on a hot summer's day in London, while I was lying exhausted on the floor of my flat looking up through the skylight. A classic UFO, disk-shaped and metallic-looking, flew slowly past. I followed its progress until it passed out of sight behind houses. No, it was not a balloon. What was it then? As a qualified expert on the subject (by virtue of my 1967 book *The Flying Saucer Vision*) my conclusions should carry weight, but all they amount to is, I haven't the slightest idea what is behind all this.

Just after the war, governments suspected they were secret weapons, made by German scientists perhaps. The Ministry of Defence collected a huge file of UFO reports which has just been opened for public inspection. An assortment of world leaders had their own sightings – Jimmy Carter (in the company of sober and respectable officials, he emphasised); Sir Eric Gairy of Grenada, who told the United Nations assembly about it; Idi Amin, who identified the UFO he saw over Lake Victoria as a portent of good luck for Uganda. Millions of ordinary people have had similar experiences. UFOs are now commonplace and of no further interest to the media: in 2008 there was a long-lasting display of UFOs across the southern United States, massively witnessed and photographed –

but you probably never heard about it.

This world and our existence in it are totally mysterious. As in Plato's allegory of the cave, all that we see of reality is its reflections and shadows, and from these we compose the myths and fables that we live by. UFOs and their kindred phenomenon, crop circles, are effects of unknown causes, so the only level on which they can be assimilated is that of meaning.

The first writer to acknowledge this was Carl Jung in his 1959 book, *Flying Saucers*. These 'things seen in the sky' have a physical element, he said, because

In many cases, an individual sighting had developed into a full-blown visionary experience

they are detected on radar screens. But they are also of mythical nature, as agents and portents of changing times and new ways of thinking. Jung's boldness has been amply justified. Times and thoughts have indeed changed, partly in response to the UFO presence. In many of the cases I came across during my UFO studies, an individual sighting had developed into a full-blown visionary experience. The most common remark I heard from those so affected was, 'Then I realised *we are not alone*'. That is a wide expression, covering every possible kind of entity, from extra-terrestrial visitors to angels, demons and Hermes, the god of revelation himself. Everyone has their own understanding of that realm. But above its variety of interpretations, 'we are not alone' is the triumphant cry of one who has achieved a quest, who has discovered purpose and meaning in life. The traditional key to happiness and blessings is the realisation that life extends, on every level of being, everywhere, and that, as Plato himself declared, 'Things are better taken care of than you can imagine.' Do we need UFOs to remind us of that?

JOHN MICHELL
OLDIE COLUMNIST, 1992–2009

CORNISH PILCHARD BOAT *designed and lithographed by* DAVID GENTLEMAN · *Published by J. Lyons & Co. Ltd. Printed by Chromoworks Ltd. London*

A Slice of Art
The Lyons Lithographs, 1947–1955

NICK RHODES *on the imaginative post-war corporate patronage which brought some of the finest British artists to the tea-drinking masses*

When faced with the task of improving the interiors of their teashops after the Second World War, J Lyons & Co commissioned lithographs by leading British artists, including L S Lowry, Duncan Grant and Edward Ardizzone, to decorate the 250 teashops.

The Lyons directors responsible for the teashops were aware of the successful advertising posters produced by the fuel company Shell-Mex in the 1930s, and they employed Jack Beddington, artistic director at Shell-Mex, to co-ordinate a similar scheme for Lyons. Barnett Freedman, an artist and leading printmaker, was recruited to oversee the technical aspects of the project, and the renowned printers, Chromoworks Ltd, were engaged to print the lithographs. In 1947 the first series of sixteen Lyons lithographs was published, and two further series of twelve prints followed in 1951 and 1955.

Thirty-two of the original forty prints went on display in 2008 in an exhibition at the South Kensington and Chelsea Mental Health Centre, organised by the Nightingale Project, a charity which takes art and music into hospitals. Stephen Barnham, the show's curator, had long had a passion for this period of British art, and he put together the largest collection of Lyons lithographs to be exhibited in London for over thirty years.

LEFT: Cornish Pilchard Boat by David Gentleman (Third Series, 1955)   TOP: Albert Bridge by Carel Weight (First series, 1947)   RIGHT: The Dolls at Home by Edward Bawden (First series, 1947)   BELOW: The Bird Cage by William Scott (First series, 1947)   BELOW RIGHT: An Illustration of a Lyons tearoom by Peter Bailey

The Dedham Reds

Communism, nude sunbathing and vegetarian dogs – it's not surprising that the habits of **DAVID LOSHAK**'s *family raised eyebrows in the small village of Dedham...*

David Loshak (right) and his family in Dedham, c. 1945

Within a month of VE Day, my mother, sister and I returned from five years in New York as wartime evacuees to rejoin my father at our bomb-damaged home in the Vale of Dedham – Constable country.

I was twelve.

We did not exactly fit in. Dedham was a citadel of God-fearing respectability, stiff-necked Toryism, prelapsarian virtue, feudalistic forelock-tugging, prudery and conventional anti-semitism. My 37-year-old father was a vocal member of the Communist Party. A formidable six-footer, he affected a Chekhovian beard. Educated at St Paul's, finishing school in Switzerland and the LSE, he was an object of suspicion – 'an intellectual.' He earned a living of sorts by selling antiquarian books. He wore green shirts. We were Jewish. We were atheists. My diminutive mother wore slacks. Our car was not a stolid Morris or a stately Armstrong Siddeley, but a snazzy Citroën coupé with a sexy dicky seat. On principle, my parents shopped where the tied-cottage families shopped, at the Co-op, not the swanky grocery opposite the church. And they were 'cranks' – followers of 'nature cure' and its diet of salads and nut cutlets which, after five years of milk shakes, cherry sodas and hamburgers, I endured daily. Zabac and Zilla, our two great Danes, suffered a similar vegetarian regimen, though they were mercifully spared the regular enemas recommended by the monthly 'food reform' journal, *Health for All*. These were administered to me by my father's nubile wartime mistress. At other times, she walked the garden topless.

The adults' *ménage à trois* enjoyed nude sunbathing. There were weekend house parties where discussions on dialectical materialism by day and recitals by my mother on the Steinway of an evening culminated in the creaking floors of both staircases and squeaky doors along the corridors at night. Thus began my sex education.

In July, the first general election for ten years produced a Labour landslide. Our fresh-faced new MP, Charles Smith (later Lord Delacourt Smith), one of our house guests, was not merely left-wing but an avowed 'fellow-traveller' – a Communist sympathiser; possibly even, it was whispered, a 'secret' member of 'the Party'. In Dedham village, the tweedy colonels and their frosty ladies prepared to leave the country for fear of Clem Attlee's tumbrils turning up to take them to the guillotine.

As we now had a Red for an MP, what better for 'the Party' than to pull off a similar trick at local level? My father stood for election to Dedham parish council.

There was nothing new about elected parish councils – they had been introduced by Gladstone's Local Government Act of 1894 – but in Dedham there had never really been one. For the five ensuing decades, Dedham's gentry had shrewdly stitched things up to provide a self-selecting benevolent dictatorship of twelve (all men, of course) which was regularly 're-elected' unopposed without the bother and expense of a secret ballot. At 'parish meetings' every three years, a few submissive yokels dutifully gave their acquiescence to these cosy squirearchical arrangements.

1945, though, was different. It was the village hall, not the council, that was packed. The candidates were announced – the twelve sitting members plus the beardie in the front row. 'Any questions?'

asked the chairman. There was just one. 'Can Mr Loshak tell us,' brayed a cut-glass voice, 'whether he is foreign-born?' Before my Hackney-born father could reply, the chairman, with proper Tory rectitude, slapped the inquisitor down.

On polling day, my father came in 12th – Dedham's first (and undoubtedly last) Communist, Jewish, atheist, food-reforming, colour-shirted, free-loving parish councillor. 'I will want "Harry Loshak – He Served Dedham" on my tombstone,' he declared over the nut cutlets that evening.

Though supremely self-assured (indeed mired) in Marxist certitude, my father was uncharacteristically edgy when preparing for the meeting of the newly elected council. How would he be received by such daunting notables as Mr Clover, the chairman, who owned Dedham Mill; the Establishment's favourite architect, Sir Raymond Erith; and the nobs who rode with the peppery Sir Alfred Munnings, president of the Royal Academy? Years later, Mr Clover's

On polling day, my father became Dedham's first (and last) Communist, Jewish, atheist, free-loving parish councillor

son, Charles, the *Daily Telegraph*'s environment correspondent, told me (by then writing leaders for that 'reactionary rag') that his father had told him how uneasy they had felt about the looming confrontation with the fire-eating Bolshevik.

The meetings were, of course, utterly apolitical, concerned with ponds, ditches, drainage and footpaths. The revolution was amicably postponed.

Nevertheless, my dad attracted the attention of the authorities. Our phone, on a sideboard in the dining room, was kept covered by a tea cosy at mealtimes because my father believed (though I did not, and years later learned that I was wrong) that it was 'tapped'. Officers from the Special Branch called by one afternoon. They asked to look at my father's personal library. It was suspiciously well stocked with dodgy literature – alongside Dickens (very popular in the Soviet Union), Thackeray and Trollope, next to Shakespeare and Sheridan, was Shaw (admirer of Stalin); beside Wordsworth and Keats were Byron the libertine and Shelley the anarchist. Nearer the bone were naughty Sir Alan Herbert, banned Olympia Press paperbacks smuggled in

from Paris, and books by D H Lawrence which no one else in Dedham, certainly, would wish their wives or servants to read. Worse still, Marie Stopes and Krafft-Ebing nestled alongside four fat volumes of sexology by Havelock Ellis. But, most damning of all, filling a bookcase by the French windows, together with the pale pink covers of the Left Book Club and many costive Marxist tomes, were the Complete Works of Lenin. Ah ha! The flatfoots doggedly browsed. After earnest cogitation, they took away the most subversive book of all: the Complete Works of Oscar Wilde.

And then came 1946. Our East Anglian backwater settled into the dreary routines of the 20th century's dullest decade, when the now unremembered Minister of Food, Sir Ben Smith, brought bacon and poultry rations lower than during the war, withdrew dried egg supplies completely, and urged us to eat snoek. And, as the full scale of the 'Final Solution' was coming to light, a Dedham boy called me 'dirty Jew'.

Decades later, my parents dead, my sister and I installed a bench overlooking Dedham Vale inscribed with their names and the dates they had lived there. Within a month, it was vandalised. We had it repaired. Within a month, again, it was torn out, towed away and smashed. Even in death, it seems, Harry and Judith Loshak did not exactly fit in.

'This one didn't work'

RANT

COMPUTERS SEEM to be destroying literacy. Any imbecile who has learned to type thinks he can write.

I constantly get correspondence from so-called 'students' at so-called 'universities' who cannot write the simplest letter.

They have never heard of terms of address such as Dear Mr or Dear Sir. Their letters begin: 'Hi.' There's no address and no date. Sometimes the entire letter is written in texting style with 'I' and other capitalised words in lower case. Usually there is no punctuation whatsoever.

Having typed out this garbage, they don't read it through. One imbecile writes: 'i would really like a signed of you if possible signed to Michael.' He has left out the very thing he is asking for! But at least he has capitalised his own name.

Another halfwit wrote to my agent asking her to forward his letter to me but forgot to mention my name. The secretary managed to work out who he had in mind. He says he is an illustration student and talks about 'illustraded books', being an 'illustrater' and 'storys'. He says he is sending out questionnaires, but at the end adds a PS: 'sorry i forgot to attach my questionnaire.'

Can these cretins really be at a UNIVERSITY? If so, the word 'university' has lost all meaning. No wonder the students prefer to say they are at 'uni'. Not a bad word for it.

Years ago there was an unpleasant term, no longer in use: ESN – Educationally Sub-Normal. Maybe it is time to revive it, but to use it now for the institutions, not the people. Educationally Sub-Normal Universities?

RAYMOND BRIGGS

ILLUSTRATION BY TOM PLANT

Charles Wheeler

When the veteran foreign correspondent **CHARLES WHEELER** *died in 2008, there was no shortage of tributes praising his distinguished career as a reporter. Here* **JANE GARDAM** *recalls how Charles's professionalism and dedication were not confined to events on the world's stage – small things mattered too*

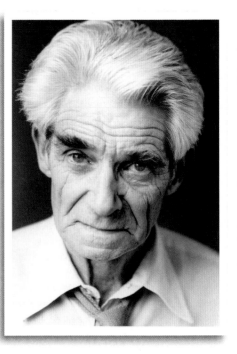

I met Charles Wheeler at a wedding anniversary party where almost every face was famous and the assembled IQ of the guests was enough to daunt Einstein. They were gathered in from the grandees of television and radio, political commentators, *Panorama*, *Newsnight*, the BBC World Service, foreign correspondents. I was there primarily to keep an eye on my seven-year-old granddaughter and her friends who were for some reason trying to hide wine bottles under trestle tables.

Probably because they hadn't hidden mine, I asked Charles Wheeler, who had sat down next to me, if he would come and talk to the smallest Arts Society in the world on the Solway Firth, where I have been patron since Melvyn Bragg (born there but rather busier than me) retired. It functions in a pub near an almost obliterated village, thirty miles from the Lake District. This pub stands on mild green land where my father's family has farmed in a small way for over 150 years. Solway Arts is run by a passionate group of mostly retired teachers and has been struggling on for half a century. It battles to keep its tiny Arts Council grant.

'Nobody from the South will come,' I said. 'The less famous they are the more likely they are not even to reply to an invitation.'

'I'll come,' said Charles Wheeler and he took out his diary. 'Yes, I could come that Saturday. I'll be flying in from Prague in the morning and whatever happens I mustn't miss the plane to Hamburg on the Monday, but I'm quite free over the Saturday night.' He must have been about 75 at the time.

I said, 'It's a long train ride to West Cumberland and it will be the weekend. The trains are awful. And we don't offer much of a fee.' (£200!!)

'I don't want a fee or travel expenses. I'll come.'

So that autumn we stood in the dark on Penrith station awaiting his train. The ruins of Penrith castle stood up behind us, like Kosovo. We hoped it might make him feel at home. The Lake District mountains were to the west. It was a lashing, stormy night. The train arrived and then left.

The platform was empty.

'Hasn't come.'

But there he was with his beautiful wife, their scrap of luggage at their feet and dragging hard on cigarettes, recently forbidden to passengers on British Rail. They were looking rather stunned.

And more stunned when we reached the pub in the fields. A smell of chips floated out over the yard, old beer seeped out of the stone walls. Cumbrians do not easily show reverence and only about seven people were lounging about inside.

'Hello, Charles. Good to see you.'

We ate a fry-up round a table and I saw for a second the unconquered jawline fall. Was this going to be all there was? Then he singled out a very young man sitting opposite, the only one there who looked shy, and began to ask him how he planned to pass his life. In five

'You want a gap year. From what exactly?'

minutes the boy was talking and Charles listened. His wife sat like a bird of paradise in a farmyard, and yet at home anywhere.

Then we all tramped down a scurvy passage into 'the hall', a room, capacity circa fifty, crammed with over a hundred. Some standing elbow-to-elbow at the back, expectant as the army. Silent. Charles began his talk.

After five minutes he removed his jacket. After ten off came his tie. Questions came fast and he answered them all as on the dreadful day of judgement.

'Who are you?' he asked one persistent person. 'Not from the BBC are you?'

'Yes. I came down from Edinburgh.'

'Good God!' said Charles 'what have I said?'

But everything he said was exact, fearless and his own.

We took them away around eleven o'clock. It was thirty miles to where we were staying the night on Ullswater. On winding roads, through tossing black trees, we came upon a car standing

I asked Charles Wheeler, who had sat down next to me, if he would come and talk to the smallest Arts Society in the world on the Solway Firth. 'I'll come,' he said

without lights on the road ahead.

'Stop!' shouts Charles. 'Someone in trouble.' He jumps out, knocks on the windows. 'Anyone there? Are you OK?'

He jumps back in. 'Loving couple,' he says, 'but best to check.'

We had another dinner. We all went to bed about two in the morning. We woke to the lake lapping, its water flickering on our bedroom ceilings. The Wheelers were already up, smoking on the terrace. The train we put them on at Penrith looked very doubtful. Somebody told me later that they had had seven changes to get back home. I never dared ask if he caught the plane to Hamburg.

Charles took no fee. He wrote me a real letter saying thank you and we always kept in touch at Christmas. He worked at everything he thought important until he dropped.

Solway Arts will not forget him.

NOT MANY DEAD
Important stories you may have missed

Police were called to a field by a worried motorist after she spotted a 'dead' horse lying on the ground, which officers found was actually asleep.
Daily Telegraph

The Duchess of Cornwall yesterday showed a nose for Chilean wine during the Royal couple's South American trip. She sampled an organic red and pronounced it 'very good'.
Daily Telegraph

TV chef Gordon Ramsay had to stop at a pub on his way to Bridlington Spa to use the toilet. 'We were absolutely gobsmacked. He turned up out of the blue and asked my wife, Katie, if he could use the loo.'
Sunday Times

Dr Who star David Tennant is enjoying a break from acting and is spending it getting furniture for his new home
Mail on Sunday

Repairs are to be made to seven high-street litter bins.
Isle of Wight County Press

Class 170 No. 170117 passed through Ipswich mid-morning on September 13, carrying a 'Not in Service' display.
The Railway Magazine

Piers Morgan has shown he has a softer side. A tub of 'Nivea for Men' moisturiser – with a touch of tanning – was spotted in his dressing room.
Metro

Frome firefighters used washing-up liquid to rescue a man whose arm was stuck in a letterbox. The man did not have any injuries.
Somerset Standard

South West Tory Euro MP Dr Caroline Jackson could have been killed or seriously injured if the European Parliament had been in session the day the roof fell in last month, an official inquiry has revealed.
Bristol Evening Post

Daniel Radcliffe, of Harry Potter fame, has said that he sometimes has trouble tying his shoelaces because he suffers from dyspraxia.
Daily Telegraph

The Duke of Edinburgh, 82, stalled his Land Rover as he arrived in church in Sandringham, Norfolk, with the Queen.
The Sun

Daughter of the forest

The remarkable **WINIFRED FOLEY** *died in March 2009, aged 94. Her first book, 'A Child in the Forest', written in her sixties, documented her extraordinary girlhood in the Forest of Dean. In this poignant 2007 interview,* **SARAH SHANNON** *asked Winifred about her first forays into writing, the hunger she endured as a child and the Iraq war...*

L ike all the best eureka moments, Winifred Foley's began under an apple tree. She was working as a labourer, picking up fallen apples, when the strain of bending to the ground made her back seize up.

A neighbour lent her the *Countryman* magazine to help her pass away her invalid hours, and she found herself riveted by its descriptions of country characters. Without any further thought, she dashed off a portrait of her beloved granny and sent it to the magazine. Six weeks later, when she had long forgotten her creative impulse, she received a letter from the *Countryman*. They would pay her six guineas to publish her pen portrait – a fortune for a labourer who received 1/9d an hour picking apples. At the age of sixty, Winifred's writing career had begun.

Her next foray was a short piece about her childhood in the 1920s, written in response to an advertisement in the *Radio Times*. Once again, her beautifully written reminiscences attracted attention. The BBC invited her to speak on television and to her astonishment a fellow guest was Laurie Lee. 'I couldn't believe I was in the same room as the man who'd written *Cider with Rosie*. My children had brought that book home from school and I absolutely loved it.' What was he like? 'Well,' Winifred pauses, delicately. 'He'd

had too much to drink.'

Now 92, Winifred lives in Cheltenham. Dressed in neatly pressed trousers and a blouse, her white hair cropped in a tidy bob, she looks like any other older resident of that spa town. But her small twinkling eyes and wide smile hint at the intelligence and

'Something came over me that day in the forest. I cannot describe it. I had this strange feeling of detachment'

humour of this writer whose memoirs and novels have delighted readers for the past three decades.

Her first book is probably her best known. *A Child in the Forest* [recently reprinted as *Full Hearts and Empty Bellies*] was commissioned by BBC

Books following that early television appearance and went on to inspire a television drama, a play and a series of *Woman's Hour* adaptations.

It describes her life as a young girl in the Forest of Dean, cut off from the outside world by its geographical remoteness and scarcely touched by the 20th century's innovations. The ten by twenty miles of secluded forest contained families who had lived there for generations and who spoke a dialect that was quite unique.

Her family fetched its water from a well. Her mother laboured to get through their washing using a dolly tub and, later, a mangle. Hygiene and germs weren't words Winifred ever heard used at home. Baths were very infrequent. Electricity didn't reach her tiny cottage during her childhood but a candle and paraffin lamp sufficed.

Little wonder that her village stayed much the same as it had been in the previous century; it didn't even have a road connecting it to other villages. Instead Winifred would wander along woodland paths in the shadow of the mighty oaks, and the forest itself becomes one of her book's strongest characters. She felt its powerful place in her life even as a young girl. 'When I was about eight years old I remember walking with a jug and a penny to buy milk. I loved walking through the trees. Something came over me that day. I cannot describe it. I had this strange feeling of detachment. The forest was so beautiful and I felt so insignificant.

It took me a while to come back to myself. It stuck with me for the rest of my life, that strange feeling,' she says.

Perhaps the most shocking part of Winifred's account is her family's battle against hunger. She recalls the frequent niggling ache of their empty bellies, the bread and dripping that made up most of their poor diet, and she describes in lip-smackingly sumptuous detail the occasions when a kindly teacher or relative treated her to a piece of ham or a cream cake.

Like many autobiographies, Winifred's book caused a rift in her family. Her older sister Bess resented the graphic descriptions of their childhood poverty.

'I can only put it down to jealousy, unfortunately. My older sister was very clever and beautiful; you wouldn't think she was my sister at all. She took umbrage because I wrote about the poverty even though all our friends and neighbours knew about it.'

In her eighties, Winifred decided to write her first novel. Now she's writing her fifth. Based loosely on the characters and events she recalls from her early years, the stories have been immensely popular. 'There must be something in them because they do sell out. It's an unbelievable feeling that there are people out there who want to read my books.

'Four of my children went through grammar school and two of them have got degrees. I only went to the village school and so my writing has taken everybody aback, including me.'

Her writing methods are as spare and simple as her prose. She writes on an A4 notepad in scrawling longhand. The idea of a typewriter or, heaven forbid, a computer is alien to her. As chunks of the novel get written she sends them off to a niece in Denmark who types them up and sends them to her publisher. Sadly, she insists her current work-in-progress, a romance based in a Jewish household in the East End of London, will be her last.

'I rush through it too much these days but that's because I think I'm going to peg out before I finish. I shan't do any more books after this. I've run out of ideas.' Winifred shows no regret that her writing career began so late in a life marked by hard work and poverty. 'I was so busy bringing up my four children, working on the land and before that going charring. I'd have had no time for writing back then.'

While many struggle to remember the events of the past decade, Winifred calls up freshly minted images from almost a century ago. She has a simple but intriguing explanation for her clarity of recall. 'At fourteen years old we were sent away from home into service. I'd never been on a proper bus. I knew nothing about streets or house numbers and then I arrived in London.

'Oh, I was so homesick. All I did was think about home and everything about it became precious. When you're torn away from something it becomes so much more important. I sometimes get letters from girls at my school and they also jog my memory, so I think it's a common reaction if you get sent away to remember something well.'

Writing became a form of therapy for Winifred in her eighties when she lost her beloved husband Syd, a fiercely intelligent man whom she first met on a march against Oswald Mosley. 'We could talk about anything under the sun. We would argue and try to influence each other's opinions. Since he's died it's been absolutely dreadful.

'There's a kind of loneliness that only old people know about. We're handicapped in our own bodies. If I could go for a walk or do a day's work I'd feel so much better. Half of us go cuckoo.'

Despite these words, Winifred cannot be a melancholic figure for long. Soon she hoots with laughter over her secret fascination with the *Daily Mail*'s neurotic columnist Liz Jones. 'When will she boot her husband out?' Winifred asks with girlish glee. Quickly she moves onto her anti-war sentiments, sparked almost a century ago by the First World War and still as strongly in evidence today, as she rails against Tony Blair and his involvement in Iraq: 'I think war is an obscenity. How can that Tony Blair walk about after what he's done by going to war in Iraq? He gives a noble reason for it but it's rubbish. Two of my children went up to London to march against the war.'

As she talks to me in her pretty sitting room, Winifred breaks off to urge me to eat more cake and biscuits, or to have another cup of tea. She won't tolerate the ache of hungry bellies any more. Finally, on parting, she tries to push more food into my hand for the journey. What is it? An apple, of course.

'I've put in a water feature...'

Olden life

What was...
The Bird?

'THERE'S A Bird about,' I remember an old actor-Johnny saying during a theatre interval, as he looked up at the gallery which had been restive and emitting the odd hoot. He sniffed the air as if he could smell it. A shaken Sir John Gielgud made no bones about it. 'This was Bird – undoubted Bird,' he said during the tour of *Veterans*. 'They can't bear to hear me say "Shit" in my gorgeous voice. A man in Brighton got up and shouted, "Don't say that word in front of my wife!"'

'Dear boy, I have got the Bird many times,' Noël Coward informed me. 'After the first night of *Sirocco* I was spat upon as well at the stage door. I had to send my tailcoat to the cleaners.'

In days when no one is allowed to shout 'Boo!' for fear of prosecution, getting the Bird is almost forgotten in the theatre. Audiences used not to be content to sit in polite boredom in the dark and quietly go to sleep. At the very least they got up and left, and not without loudly voicing their opinion of the proceedings first. The snap of stalls springing upright to shouts of 'Rubbish!' or 'A disgrace to the Court!' was a common accompaniment to avant garde plays at the Royal Court.

The RSC was not immune in its London seasons of contemporary plays. There was one ill-chosen Cuban ground-breaker in which an actor who had committed a murder was required to stagger about with a dripping knife and the unfortunate line, 'But what shall I do with the knife?' 'Stick it in the author!' was the inevitable reply from the upper circle.

Celebrated playwrights have known something close to the Bird. The early performances of *Waiting for Godot* in London were a by-word for the number of patrons who left and announced that they refused to wait *any longer*. When *Look Back in Anger* was revived in the West End, a woman spectator walked down the aisle to the foot of the stage and interrupted one of Jimmy Porter's tirades with a rebuke for his self-indulgence and a demand for her money back (she got it). Osborne's 'musical', *The World of Paul Slickey*, was deservedly hooted into oblivion, and Joe Orton's *What the Butler Saw* ended its first performance in a hubbub of hostility, with an aghast Ralph Richardson visibly wondering how he had ever got into it.

Booing and catcalling is a time-honoured theatre tradition. Kean was often jeered off the stage. Macready was pelted with eggs. Henry James never got over the wounding rejection he received from *Guy Domville*'s first-night audience. The saintly Abbey Theatre in Dublin rioted at *The Playboy of the Western World* and *The Plough and the Stars*.

I have never witnessed fruit or eggs thrown at a straight play, but this was a common hazard for 18th- and 19th-century players. But above all, they hissed. Ladies of fashion hissed through their fans in order not to look ugly – and that is why it was called the Bird. The bird referred to was a goose. You would have a job nowadays to catch the Bird anywhere. A pity, in my view. Booing is as legitimate as cheering; hissing is simply the opposite of applause – and no actor I know has ever complained about getting a round. And there are beneficial effects. Peter Ustinov's unendurable play, *No Sign of the Dove*, got the Bird as early as the second act: it ended when he walked on to be received in uproar. He later said any playwright should have the experience – once.

We are constantly urged to indulge in bogus audience participation via some silent website. Bring back the Bird, I say. Theatre pros never see they have a turkey on their hands until a paying audience tells them so. The pity is one can't boo television.

PETER LEWIS

Modern life

What is...
Risk Assessment?

THE HEALTH and Safety industry has spawned a multitude of ludicrous stories that have in turn entertained us or caused us to wring our hands in despair. But nothing is quite as batty as the pseudo-science of the Risk Assessment, and nothing quite as depressing as the amount of time and effort expended in compiling the reams of paperwork such documents demand.

This is how most Risk Assessments (RAs) work: the organiser of the activity in question has to evaluate each component of the task in hand and allocate two scores, usually on a scale of one to four. The first score is their assessment (i.e. guess) of the probability of an accident taking place – one means it is improbable, four means it is near certain to occur, and so on. The second figure measures the severity of the outcome on the same scale, from a minor scrape to major injury or death. RA forms have a grid for each sub-activity, and a final column in which the two scores are multiplied together. Thus a score of 16 (i.e. 4 x 4) indicates a near certainty of disaster, presumably reserved for suicide missions. The logic for this arbitrary arithmetic

'Quick! One of this lot is about to have their hopes and dreams blown apart!'

The amount of time and effort expended in compiling the reams of paperwork for a risk assessment is totally batty

Two tales of risky business...

A MAJOR utility company, facing an investigation by the Environment Agency, had queried where a tape-recorded interview with its employee should take place. These are verbatim extracts from the EA's replies: 'I am unable to arrange for the interview to be conducted at your own offices. It would be remiss of me to put my officer's health and safety at risk... We have identified that the conduct of interviews is a high-risk activity for our officers...

'Of course, we could bring extra tapes, spare machine, etc. to your offices. However, in order to protect my officer's health and safety, it is not practical or safe to carry this amount of equipment with them.'

WHEN THE BBC needed a temporary receiving aerial on a tower block in the City for a one-day seminar, it seemed a simple matter to send a man up in the lift to attach the small magnetic base – essentially a car aerial and worth about £15 – to one of the many metal air-conditioners or steel components in the plant area on the roof.

And so it proved, except that the building managers demanded an application form, a health and safety policy, a high height working certificate, a method statement and a Risk Assessment. The Beeb had to hire an outside contractor at a cost of £250 to carry out the five-minute task – and to compile the fourteen pages of detailed documentation required to obtain the necessary permission.

remains a mystery; there could equally be columns for the phase of the moon or the direction of the wind, and the maths could just as well involve addition, elevation to the nth power or integral calculus. Finally, another column is provided for the assessor to write in the appropriate precautionary measure.

Risk Assessments have penetrated the deepest corners of everyday life. Teachers, for example, cannot carry out any activity with their classes more dangerous than sitting still and facing the front without one. Ordinary trips away from school (never mind adventure activities) require individually compiled RAs. Realising that this might be a disincentive for teachers to organise trips, some public attractions are helpfully publishing pro-forma RAs to ease the process. Each sub-activity on offer has to have its own analysis of the risks. Here are a few examples picked at random from one local authority's website:

One museum entertains its younger visitors with 'traditional stories and nursery rhymes'; the hazards, rather oddly, are identified as 'poking with mask sticks or tripping on long skirts'. Risk and severity are each assessed at two, with a suggested precaution of 'Verbal warning, one-to-one close supervision'.

In the garden of another attraction,

'bee stings' are identified as a hazard – happily only a 2 x 1 score – and 'verbal instructions about bees and their habits' were recommended. A country park assesses the danger of 'slipping and falling' as a 2 x 1 and helpfully suggests 'verbal warning: no running'. By contrast, the city museum is a positive minefield; whilst the loos rank a measly 1 x 1, the revolving doors offer the young visitor an exciting frisson of danger at 2 x 3, bettered only by the sculp-

ture workshop that delivers a potentially deadly 2 x 4. To what appalling dangers we unthinkingly subjected our children in the years before Health'n' Safety was invented!

Below is a not-untypical risk assessment. I'm serious – I have been obliged in the past to prepare RAs barely less ludicrous than this for projects I have been involved in...

RODDY GYE

ACTIVITY	POTENTIAL HAZARD	PROB	SEV	RISK FACTOR	CONTROL MEASURE
• Purchasing The Oldie	Tripping at newsagent	1	3	3	Avoid buying in icy conditions
• Opening magazine	Paper cut	1	1	1	Wear gloves to open
• Reading page 5	Damage to eyesight	2	3	6	Wear glasses for small print
• Looking at cartoons	Risk of hyperventilation	2	2	4	Keep paper bag nearby
• Reading article on health and safety	Risk of apoplexy	3	4	12	Have ambulance on standby before reading

David Stoten

Every year since 2006, artist **DAVID STOTEN** *has caricatured the winners of The Oldie of the Year Awards.* **NICK NEWMAN** *tells us a little bit about the man behind the faces*

I first met David Stoten when working with Ian Hislop as a writer for Spitting Image in the early 1980s. David, who had previously worked for British MAD magazine, had been taken on by Roger Law and Peter Fluck to draw caricatures and create sculptures for the show. Together with the seemingly infant Tim Watts and the Argentinian refugee Pablo Bach, he was the core of the Spitting Image artistic team, under Roger and Peter's art school-like direction. David's talent was enviable and prodigious. I remember him skimming through news video tapes, speedily drawing sketches of his victims which would later transform into the life-size puppets which became a staple of TV satire in the 80s and early 90s. Later, he turned his seemingly limitless artistic talents to animation – and was nominated for an Oscar for his and Watts's brilliant short film The Big Story – featuring three Kirk Douglases. This BAFTA-winning short supported Quentin Tarantino's Pulp Fiction – and easily stole the show. Since then he's worked as a storyboard artist and animator – and a couple of years ago he, Tim Watts, Ian Hislop and I collaborated on a James Bond animation project which has sadly yet to be realised. However, it served as a reminder that Stoten is one of the finest caricaturists working today. Enjoy.

ABOVE, clockwise from left: Terry Wogan, Terry Pratchett, Vince Cable, John Sergeant. BOTTOM RIGHT – BACK ROW: Eileen Atkins, Ian Paisley. FRONT ROW, l–r: David Hockney, Moira Stuart, Ros Altmann and Stanley Baxter. BOTTOM LEFT: Diana Athill and Andrew Sachs. INSET, clockwise from left: Walter Wolfgang, Carol Thatcher, Admiral Sir Alan West, Camilla, Duchess of Cornwall, Sandra Howard, George MacDonald Fraser, Alan Whicker

His final parish

> " I have crawled out at last far as I dare on to a bough of country that is suspended between sky and sea "

In 1978 **R S THOMAS**, *the great but grumpy Welsh poet, left the village of Aberdaron where he had been vicar for eleven years.* **KEN COOPER** *has been there to see how he's remembered*

Right: R S Thomas, portrait by Jane Bown
Facing page, top: St Hywyn's, the poet's old church, against the background of Aberdaron Bay

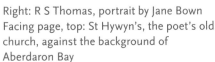

At the very tip of North Wales, beyond Snowdonia, beyond even Anglesey, the road runs finally down to Aberdaron. It's a tumble of whitewashed cottages and grey slate roofs, where the Lleyn Peninsula points a rocky finger into the Irish Sea. The road is narrow, the hedgerows are high and tangled with fuchsia and honeysuckle. For more than a thousand years, it has been the old pilgrim route to Bardsey Island, an outpost of Celtic spirituality and a stepping-stone to heaven.

In 1967 R S Thomas arrived as the new vicar of Aberdaron. The parish was like the man himself – remote, craggy and close to the elements. Thomas was introspective, often grumpy and difficult, yet he created some of our most bleakly beautiful verse – work that would earn him a Nobel Prize nomination. It was an ideal place for a poet who wrote of the wild landscape and hard lives of the Welsh hill people.

The wind goes over the hill pastures
Year after year, and the ewes starve,
Milkless, for want of the new grass.
And I starve, too, for something the spring
Can never foster in veins run dry.

In his eleven years at Aberdaron, some of the villagers found him distant, even downright rude. Others were touched by his gruff acts of kindness. He taught the local children bird-watching and, bizarrely, croquet. And all the time, his poetry was growing in

reputation. Sir John Betjeman wrote in the preface to a book of Thomas's verse that his own name 'will be forgotten long before that of R S Thomas'. He won the 1964 Queen's Gold Medal for Poetry, ranking him with W H Auden, Philip Larkin and Ted Hughes.

It's thirty-odd years since he retired and left the village, but he's still very much part of the Aberdaron landscape. At the Eleri Stores, Gareth Jones sells some of his books every day: 'Yes, they're on constant order, and sales have been steadily going up. A few years ago a busload of Chinese students pulled up outside and bought virtually my entire stock of Thomas books. He's definitely one of Aberdaron's attractions.' But at the Post Office and Spar stores,

He learned Welsh in his late twenties, but decided it was too late to use it in his verse

John Williams disagrees: 'I knew him a long time ago. He was cold and short-tempered, not a very pleasant person. Yes, he's written some poems and brought in some tourists, but he's like van Gogh – more popular since he died.'

Thomas would have hated the idea that he'd brought trippers into Wales. He was a fierce Welsh nationalist, and he hoped his new and remote parish would be a place of national purity. He learned Welsh in his late twenties, but decided it was too late in life to use it in his verse.

Where can I go, then, from the smell
Of decay, from the putrefying of a dead
Nation? I have walked the shore
For an hour and seen the English
Scavenging among the remains
Of our culture, covering the sand
Like the tide and, with the roughness
Of the tide, elbowing our language
Into the grave that we have dug for it.

The Rev Jim Cotter is the current vicar of Aberdaron: 'I think his motive for coming here was to find somewhere untainted by the English. To him they were the destroyers of innocence. He was a bit of a reluctant pastor – more in tune with nature and farm life than with interacting with people. But he did a lot of good by stealth. And he'd often pop in for tea with his elderly parishioners, then quietly leave a loaf of bread he'd baked.'

We're sitting in his old church, St. Hywyn's, listening to the steady soft roar of the sea a few yards away. There is a deep sense of timelessness and peace, and it's hard to imagine here that Thomas could find his God so remote and unresponsive. There are two naves – the original Norman, and a second from around 1500, added as a hostel for pilgrims waiting for the Bardsey Island ferry. The church is low and humble, like the barns in the local fields. The roof is timbered, and plain glass windows look out on the graveyard, the sky and the sea.

There's a little R S Thomas exhibition on the vestry wall, and a shop selling candles, prayer cards and copies of his work. Here, at the very tip of the Lleyn peninsula, he must have felt as deep into Wales as he could be – and as far

from the English. But more than 15,000 people now visit his church every year, and thousands more come for the walking and the scenery. Today it's the tourists, especially the English, who bring in much of Aberdaron's money.

The peninsula is little more than a mile wide here and the sea is an ever-present force. The journey is a long one – something of a pilgrimage for the visitors, and for Thomas himself, grumbling about escaping them:

I have crawled out at last
far as I dare on to a bough
of country that is suspended
between sky and sea.

His biographer, Byron Rogers, called him the loneliest man he'd ever met. One of his successors, the Rev Evelyn Davies, said, more cheeringly, that as a poet he gave us 'the words we need, but could not bring forth, to express our own spiritual struggle and our own rare glimpses of joy.'

'It's funny – everyone always remembers where they were when Humpty Dumpty had a great fall'

Whiteboard jungle

Kate Sawyer has been teaching in a comprehensive school for ten years. What awaited her when she first started was very much a surprise...

I went into teaching because I loved English Literature and felt I could change, if not the world, then the lives of children otherwise not introduced to books. I sincerely and passionately believed that everyone's life could be altered by Shakespeare and Thackeray and Trollope and Coleridge.

I did not know that in the English state-school system no one even looks at Coleridge and only the very dedicated teacher will encourage or even allow their students to read a whole 19th-century novel. (They read chapters 1, 14 and 22 of *Great Expectations* and discuss how Dickens creates atmosphere. Of course they also watch the film so they can refer to the rest of the story and it looks as though the book has been read.)

I went into teaching hoping that I would become a Head of Department and would be able to point students ever deeper into our literary heritage.

I did not know that Heads of Department spend more time with statistics than books. That they are ruled, not by *Rikki-Tikki-Tavi*, but by something called Panda Scores. That it does not matter if some children leave school unable to read and write as long as enough leave with the number of A*–C grades which will satisfy the governors, the LEA and the government.

I went into teaching believing that I could entice anyone, from whatever background, into the joys of reading.

I did not know that libraries are being ripped out of schools and replaced with 'Learning Resource Centres' – otherwise known as computer suites. With no books at home, and no books at school, there is No Chance.

I did not go into teaching because I 'loved kids'. I took a robust view of that. Some 'kids' are amusing, some are dull. Some are essentially good people and a few, like some adults, are essentially bad.

I did not guess how much the success of teachers depends on the relationships they form with the children (still not kids).

I had no idea that, as well as preparing people for exams, and yes, influencing some into loving reading and writing, I would also be called upon in many other ways. That the following years would see me handing pregnancy tests over a

Libraries are being ripped out of schools and replaced with 'Learning Resource Centres' – a.k.a. computer suites

lavatory wall, or giving a sobbing girl lessons in how to walk in a ball gown before she would leave the safety of the lavatory and join her leavers' ball. I did not know that children really do turn up to school drunk on vodka or high on crack cocaine. (In the morning, that's what seems so odd. Most of us have the odd tipple but eight thirty seems very early in the morning for a vice.) I did not know that I would witness a boy setting another

boy's hair alight, nor the euphemistic joys of report writing. I did not know that I would be standing between two boys twice my height to stop them hitting each other, or that I would spend hours and hours with children with 'pasts' (already) in the hope that if I could bully – coerce – lull – seduce – them into wanting and gaining a GCSE I might just be helping to give them a future.

I thought that I would become bored with teaching – the same books, a year as repetitive and cyclical as a farmer's, a grinding lack of room to think, or feel, or step out of line. I was wrong. Of all the careers I've had, this is the least dull. It is the most intense, and the most dramatic. It is closer to acting than a lot of stage work. I am a different person with every class – I become whatever will engage them. I have eaten a tablespoon of mustard in front of a class to make the children work; I have danced and spun and laughed and shouted and cajoled and threatened, to make the children work. I have taught poker to prove some esoteric point. I have dressed up and dressed down, changed my accent and talked foreign languages. I have kept their secrets and sometimes told their secrets. I have done everything in my power to awaken their curiosity about the world outside their doors.

But this is not my story – this is the story of teachers all over Britain. This is the story of our battle against the bureaucrats, against each other, against – but in the end for – the children.

BORE TV
(See Digital Channel 356)
This week's highlights 4—10 February 2009

✤ DECISION
Monday 6:45pm, Bore TV

Cyril and partner Adam (above) have still to decide on their summer holiday plans for 2008. In the fourth programme of the new series Adam has sent off for a brochure for the 'gay island' of Mykonos. But Cyril has been there once before and doesn't want to be reminded of an unhappy experience with a former boyfriend. An argument flares up when he proposes Minehead. **(S) (146142)**

✤ DECISION MAKING
Tuesday 9pm, Bore TV

Once again we go backstage with the 'Decision' production team as they prepare for their latest series. Producer Jenny Pogrom (pictured) is checking through literally hours of recorded footage and picking out the highlights. And programme researchers Ros and Becky visit a Somerset vicar trying to decide whether or not to install a Satnav in his car. Is it a good enough story for the Decision gang? **(S)(155786)**

✤ TEST THE NATION – SUDOKU CHALLENGE
Hosted by Carol Vorderman
Friday 8pm, Bore TV

Play Sudoku live on air against thousands of other contestants by pressing the keys on your interactive remote. [repeat] **(S) (145192)**

✤ CAMCORDER NATION – PET SPECIAL
Wednesday 11.30pm, Bore TV

Hilarious clips of cats falling off radiators, dogs barking at microwave ovens and camels spitting at tourists. Has an animal in a petting farm recently chewed your sleeve a bit? Send us your hilarious clip – we pay £12 for each one shown. **(S)(147842)**

✤ ULTIMATE SURVIVAL
With Roy Shears
Friday 9:30pm, Bore TV

It's day six on the North Downs Way, and Roy's survival techniques are tested to the limit. He demonstrates how to construct an all-weather shelter out of an old carrier bag and a triangular plastic sandwich wrapper. But will his ancient aboriginal recipe for baked slugs help stave off the hunger pangs? **(S)(999132)**

PICK OF THE WEEK

✤ WORST EVER TAILBACKS
With Baz Slammer
Monday 7.30pm, Bore TV

Includes the first ever interview with Chuck Morgentern, 93-year-old survivor of the famous Oregon Highway Tailback of 1951, involving 10,000 vehicles and 14 fatalities. **(S)(145199)**

✤ RECYCLEWATCH
with Bill Oddie and Sally Trumpton
Friday 8pm, Bore TV

We make our daily visit to chart the progress of the composters. In Shropshire, Mr and Mrs Fulton's grass cuttings have started to mulch, while in Bloxwich our night-vision cameras pick up some exciting oxidisation occurring among Mr Briggs's vegetable peelings. Meanwhile, there is tension in North London while we wait to see whether Diane Hemmingway has imbalanced her nutrients following her heavy depositing of privet shearings. Follow the action live through the night by tuning to BBC3. **(S) (145192)**

✤ THE DIY DOCTORS
With Caspar Leapman
Friday 8:30pm, Bore TV

This week we're in Pembrokeshire, where the team help a couple who have been trying to fix their banister for over a year, a man whose loft hatch is too far to the left, and a hapless pair of newlyweds who just can't seem to get their shelves straight! **(S) (142342)**

Dinner with the Duchess

*When **PAULA KELLY** took a job as a maid for an aged Duchess, she had to cope with a jabbering parrot, a champagne dinner party – and something more shocking*

I 've only had to deal with two duchesses in my life so far and one of them was a theatre. This is the story of my brief and not entirely comfortable encounter with the other.

Let me take you back to the London of the late Fifties, that uneven plateau between the slag-pits of austerity and the lush gardens of flower-power. I was out of work as usual and ready to do almost anything when Maud at the agency said how would I fancy a duchess? 'We've got this duchess and she's just quarrelled with her companion – well more of a housemaid really – and needs somebody pronto. She lives in Kensington. Fancy the job?' I did.

The house was tall and dark and at least half of the windows were shuttered. I pulled an ancient bell. The door opened and an angular woman, dressed to go out, gave me a fierce look, as if I had been keeping her waiting. 'Yes?' she barked. 'I'm the new companion,' I said. She looked me up and down, disapproval deepening to disbelief. 'You'd better come in.'

We went down some very dark stairs to the kitchen. There was a tray with a pot of tea and sliced bread on it and some rather nice china. 'This is for 'er. I'm just orff, thank Gawd. Your uniform's on the door. Second on the right, top of the second flight of stairs. Oh and 'ere's the key to the front door. Abyssinia!' And she was gone.

The Duchess could have been anything between 89 and 123, but she spoke as if she was addressing a packed Albert Hall

I got into the uniform as best as I could – it had clearly been made for a much taller woman – picked up the tray and climbed the stairs. It wasn't difficult to find the room as a series of whoops and whistles, mixed with crazy cackling, came from behind a panelled door. I knocked. The whoops, whistles and cackling stopped. 'Who is it?' The voice was high and fairly ancient. 'Me, ma'am,' I heard myself saying, 'the new companion.' 'Come in, new companion!'

The room was in half-darkness. And looming like a white sailing ship in fog, I could just make out a figure,

sitting bolt upright in her canopied bed, and waving a skinny finger at me. 'Approach! Approach!'

'You're a bit small,' said the figure, 'but I suppose you'll have to do. You can call me "Duchess" and I shall call you "Phyllis".'

'Paula,' I said. By now I could see that the figure had inaccurately applied a good deal of lipstick and a lot of yellowing powder.

Behind and slightly above her, a blood-red parrot on an iron perch was cracking nuts.

'Put the tray down there, Phyllis.'

As I did, the parrot spat some shells over me and said something that sounded like Swahili.

'That's Evelyn,' said the Duchess. 'Called after my late husband. He had similar table manners. Can you cook, Phyllis?'

I said I could, given time.

'No time possible, Phyllis. I've got a dinner party in about an hour. I shan't bother to get up. Just the Colonel and a few very old friends. T'other Phyllis should have prepared things downstairs. Oh and my dreadful daughter might look in.'

One thing I'll say for the Duchess: there was no problem with audibility. What age she was, I couldn't tell, anything between 89 and 123, but she spoke as if she was addressing a packed Albert Hall without the aid of a microphone. I was about to register a mild objection along the lines of nobody had warned me that small and instant dinner parties would be part of the agenda, when the fire-alarm went off downstairs and the Duchess filled the house once more:

'That'll be Muriel. I don't let her have a key. Show her up, Phyllis. And tell her to take her damn boots off!'

I saw what she meant. Muriel had clearly come straight from Rotten Row. There was no question however of the boots. She was past me and cantering up the stairs before I could say 'G...' There was a lot of shouting and I decided to investigate the kitchen more thoroughly. T'other Phyllis's 'preparations' were rudimentary: a few onions had been peeled, a skinny chicken lay forlornly on a baking tray and an upturned wine-glass betrayed her other interests. A quick peep into the cellar showed a satisfying display of champagne bottles as yet untouched. This might prove to be a satisfactory substitute for haute cuisine. My time spent on the NAAFI catering committee would not have been wasted. Opening the only half bottle I could see I poured myself a glass and set to work.

The chicken was humming nicely and the bottle empty when there was another burst of shouting, a slammed door and Muriel's boots thundered downstairs, along the hall and out, slamming another door – the front one this time – behind her. Then, the sound of a bugle. I tottered upstairs. The Duchess, putting down a silver regimental bugle – another relic, I imagined, of Evelyn – said, as if nothing had happened: 'Everything all right downstairs, Phyllis? Muriel won't be staying for supper but the Colonel should be here any moment. Bring him straight up and we'll have some bubbly.'

From then on things moved swiftly. The Colonel came, towing some kind of large hunting dog behind him. He was jolly and looked as if he scarcely needed the bubbly.

'The old girl on good form this evening, Phyllis? – No, don't worry, I'll see myself up.' And he did, hunting dog at the ready. The bugle sounded again and I followed with a bottle and glasses. The Colonel and hound were both spread out among the books and 'Evelyn' had retreated a bit along his bar and was muttering. The cork and the fire-alarm went off simultaneously and this time there was a skinny middle-aged man in a mustard-coloured suit on the doorstep, carrying a vase of lilies. Behind him, limping up the steps, a woman who might once have been beautiful. 'Harold!' she cried to

'No time possible, Phyllis. I've got a dinner party in about an hour. I shan't bother to get up'

the middle-aged man, 'Assist me!' They went up together with scarcely a glance at me, and the bugle summoned more glasses and another bottle. Over the next five minutes, I got the chicken out of the oven and nicely basted, sorted the veg, and opened the door to an elderly priest, two almost-young men in military uniform, an enormously tall woman in mauve, and a cat. The cat turned out to belong to the kitchen because it went straight there. Everybody else went upstairs to the accompaniment of more bugle calls and flying bottles from me. The little room began to look like that ship's cabin in *A Night at the Opera*. 'Anyone for hard-boiled eggs!' I nearly sang out, emboldened by the champagne, but the Duchess got in first.

'What's for supper, Phyllis?!'

'Chicken, Your Highness,' I exaggerated.

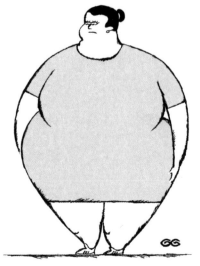

'All because the lady loves Milk Tray'

'Bring it on!' cried the Colonel.

Which I would have done, but the cat had got there first and was licking the roasted corpse vigorously. I threw one of my Dolcis shoes at it and it (the cat) vanished with a screech through the kitchen window. Rapid cosmetic surgery on the wounded bird and a mask of vegetables just about saved the situation and up the two flights of steps I went again. By now everyone in the crowded bedroom was singing. It sounded mid-way between opera and rugby football. The champagne had done its work. I brought some more and left them to it.

And very happy I was for the next hour or so. I found a battered radio on the dresser, got it to play the *Goon Show*, helped myself to some bread and cheese and another bottle from the cellar. This is the life, Phyllis, I thought. I believe the Duchess and I may have a lot in common. I shall definitely tell Maud at the agency that I'm on for tomorrow.

It wasn't, alas, to be. At about nine-thirty, the singing showing no sign of diminishing, I went up again to see if anyone fancied a nice cuppa. The Duchess appeared to be asleep against her high pillow, the priest was leading a performance of the 'Prize Song' from *Die Meistersinger* – the parrot and the hound both joining in – and one of the military men had climbed the wardrobe and was beating time with an empty champagne bottle on its mahogany crest.

No one seemed interested in tea.

I approached the Duchess. One hand was still clutching a glass of champagne, which tipped dangerously towards her alabaster bosom. I gently removed it from her grip. Or tried to. It wouldn't come loose. I gave a tug. Then another.

I put my hands on hers to prise the glass from her fingers. She was icy cold and, now I looked at her properly, her eyes were not closed at all but wide open and staring. I gave a little scream, the glass suddenly broke loose and fell to the floor with a smash. The singing stopped. The tall mauve woman said: 'Rose darling, are you all right?'

The answer was clear. Rose was no longer with us, she had moved on, she was defunct, deceased, dead. She had, as I said to Maud next morning, become my First and Last Duchess, and though the police were very nice about it, I took a train back to Birmingham the following week and found a nice quiet job in a pet shop.

Right: the memorial to Nicholas Heiney, Libby Purves' son, bears the lines from his poem *The Silence at the Song's End*

Facing page, left: letter-cutter Michael Renton cuts an inscription into slate; centre: laser-cut stainless steel lettering on a tree; right: contemporary stone in traditional heraldic style; below: the Vacher stone shows the technique of 'reverse lettering' – the text strikingly revealed by what is removed

An immoderate
SIGNIFICANCE

The bereaved often feel the need for a physical memorial – yet the decisions and processes required to bring it into being can be difficult. **LIBBY PURVES** *explains how Memorials by Artists can help*

I t is only a boulder – a giant pebble of hard porphyry shaped by some Italian river. John das Gupta, sculptor and letter-cutter in stone, found it, and saw that it would do for us. We had been a puzzle to him over the preceding months, ever since we contacted him through the agency of Harriet Frazer's 'Memorials by Artists'. Newly bereaved, we realised that the airy poetic injunction to 'break not a flower nor inscribe a stone' is a load of nonsense. Although our son Nicholas's ashes were scattered, fitly, on the wide sea that he sailed, we hungered for a memorial we could see.

So we showed das Gupta our son's poems, talked about him and took the poor man through several stages of indecision and maquettes. At first we insisted on wood (warmer, more organic) and thought about a shape based on a ship's mast. Then we changed our minds

and wanted stone (long-lasting, shining) but could not decide what shape. So, although we are bossy people who don't take help readily, it was the sculptor himself who found the boulder in a stoneyard and offered us its curves and shine; just as it was Harriet Frazer who steered us towards das Gupta in the first place. An example of his fine lettering stands in her garden in Suffolk amid a grove of work from many artists; after a death, people visit this quiet place to think about what they need.

Harriet understands the process. When she lost a beloved stepdaughter she found it difficult, in this age of machine-grinding and brisk convenience, to get a properly beautiful and unique hand-carved headstone and garden plaque. Once she had done so, she set up Memorials by Artists to link other families to the right carver. Then, realising that the old art of lettering in stone was at risk of atrophying within a generation, she founded the Memorial Arts Charity alongside the

> "...I sing inside myself
> the one wild song, song that whirls
> my words around
> until a world unfurls
> my ship's new sail"

agency. It provides workshops and an apprenticeship scheme for new young letter-cutters; and last spring, at West Dean College in Sussex, we saw the beginnings of a grander scheme: a permanent national collection of memorial art.

Why a national collection? These things are by nature personal, belonging in graveyards or individual family gardens. But when a pilot show 'The Art of Remembering' was set up at Blickling Hall in Norfolk, the response proved that families who wander among the exhibits – playful and solemn, towering or discreet, in stone, wood and metal – find it suddenly easier to talk together about their own losses and fears. We certainly did, although we never expected to need Harriet's services so soon. But we were more than glad of them. Even busy, competent, project-managing people need to take this particular task slowly and patiently, and understand that in the early stages you may envisage something you really won't want later. Some mourners begin with stiff formality, and then loosen up the style and words when the memory of the lost one's mischievousness returns. Others start out mawkish and effusive and move towards dignity. Harriet has nursed hundreds of grieving clients and patient artists through changes of emphasis, wording and design.

In the case of gravestones she also has to steer them through the maze of churchyard or council regulations about shape and size and images and words. Frankly, if you are going to be thoroughly upset by a bossy clergyman saying you can't carve a tennis racket on your daughter's gravestone because there's

no tennis in the Bible, it is handy to have an experienced advocate as go-between. And if you want a garden memorial, where nothing restricts the imagination, it helps to see the marvellous diversity of what others have done before you.

Our stone now lies beside a new-planted tree, with paths leading to it through wild grass. It bears the words of the last poem from Nicholas's book, *The Silence at the Song's End*:

> *...I sing inside myself*
> *the one wild song, song that whirls*
> *my words around*
> *until a world unfurls*
> *my ship's new sail*

The letters and lines curve and whirl with an echo of life and the sea; the moving light changes it with hours and seasons. Those who knew Nicholas bring smaller pebbles to lie around it: from gardens where he played, from his college, from lands he sailed to.

A memorial is not, as some glibly say,

a comfort. Comfort emanates from the living. The simple stone fills a different gap: its solidity makes denial impossible yet its beauty confirms that although he is gone, his having existed at all is a gift. For a thing made with a chisel it has immoderate significance.

Information

Memorials by Artists (a guide to commissioning) £12 + £2 p&p from Snape Priory, Snape, Saxmundham, Suffolk, IP17 1SA
Telephone: 01728 688934
www.memorialsbyartists.co.uk

The Art and Memory Collection, a national collection of contemporary memorial art, West Dean Gardens, West Sussex, April to November 2009

For information about Nicholas Heiney's book *The Silence at the Song's End* visit **www.songsend.co.uk**. To order for £9.95 (including UK p&p) email **songsend@mac.com** or send a cheque made payable to 'EM Purves Songsend a/c' to Songsend, Raceground Cottage, Dunwich Road, Westleton, Suffolk, IP17 3DD mentioning *The Oldie* – don't forget to include your postal address

Elegy for a Fictional Sidesman
by Kit Wright

Widely regarded
As Mynton Parish Church's

Most talented sidesman
Of the post-war period,

Eric Arthur Upton
Has handed in his plate.

Sombre and scrotal now
Hangs his collection bag,

Dark in the Vestry
In abandoned state.

Sad are the aisles
That were graced by the advent

Of his soft-shoe shuffle,
Alert yet sedate:

Mournful the heads
Of the pews where benignly

And with seamless discretion
He would stand in wait.

Highly regarded
As Mynton Parish Church's

Most finished servant
As of even date,

Eric Arthur Upton,
Boxed as a rarity,

Pauses with honour
In his own lych-gate.

Pablo Picasso

When **TRADER FAULKNER** *met* **PABLO PICASSO** *at the seaside, the great man presented him with an original – but all too ephemeral – work of fine art*

'**B**ritish actors don't dance, baby!' was Laurence Olivier's mocking response to me at Stratford in 1955, some years before he'd accepted one of his greatest challenges to hoof it as *The Entertainer*.

I had told him I felt a compulsion to learn flamenco to improve my style as an actor. My mother had been a ballerina with Diaghilev in 1911, and subsequently toured South America with Anna Pavlova. Dance held no challenging allure for me until I saw the two greatest flamenco dancers of their generations: Antonio (Ruiz Soler) and Carmen Amaya.

It took me many years to learn and I believe it was responsible for a chance encounter. Many years ago on holiday at Golf Juan in the South of France, I was riveted by a familiar figure doodling near the water's edge. Squatting on his haunches he looked exactly like a burnished brown satyr – 'well worn but worn well,' to quote the old Kiwi boot polish advert.

His gaze was compelling, and his eyes, like black opals, were fixed on a group of German oldies 'sun-baking' nearby. They were lying in a straight line, all but naked, oiled, flabby bellies, sunny-side up, like stranded, white balloons. I started to laugh. The satyr caught my eye. He spoke in French: 'You wouldn't find them amusing if you'd lived in Paris though their Nazi occupation.'

His French bore the unmistakable traces of his Andalusian origin. There was no mistaking Pablo Diego José Francisco de Paula Juan Nepomuceno María de los Remedios Crispin Crispiniano de la Santísima Trinidad Ruiz y Picasso.

'My French is very rusty,' I said. 'I'm happier with Spanish, and I can even understand Andaluz.'

'*Y cómo?*' – How come?

'I learnt to dance flamenco with the Sacromonte gypsies.'

> ## Picasso roared, 'Only in Spain could a British actor learn to dance flamenco from a paraplegic and a man with one leg'

'*Por qué?*' – Why?

I told him of my flamenco odyssey and of my lessons in Seville and Madrid with two legends, El Cojo ('The Lame One'), who had been reduced to a wheelchair by polio, and Antonio Marín, who danced with a nail in his shoe shortly after the Civil War. He contracted gangrene and, with no penicillin, had lost his leg. He had taught me to dance flamenco from the waist up, from the comfort of an armchair. Two sedentary maestros who taught me 'style' – the essence of Flamenco. I was at that time learning the rest from the greatest from that era, Antonio Gades.

Picasso roared with laughter.

'*Hómbre! Tú eres un payaso* – you're a clown. Only in Spain could a British actor learn to dance flamenco from a paraplegic and a man with one leg.'

He knelt and drew in the sand a one-legged man and me dancing wildly together. He worked like lightning with a strong, stubby, thumb, and in just a few strokes, there it was, conjured up in the sand. My likeness: unmistakable.

With a flourish he wrote '*Payaso y bailador con una pierna*' – Clown and one-legged dancer – 'Picasso.'

Then he winked. And at that moment a small wave broke across the sand – and washed the image away.

RIGHT: Trader Faulkner, Spanish Arts Festival, Sadlers Wells, 1994

Peace and tranquillity in *Laos*

Among the Buddhist temples and French colonial architecture of Laos's old capital, Luang Prabang, **JULIAN EVANS** satisfied his spiritual yearnings

In Brisbane, Australia, I spent the first six years of my life in realms of gross pleasure. Everything around me – the house with a banana plantation and an aviary of budgerigars, the never-faltering Queensland sunshine – represented life as it should be, and I only saw slowly, long after my mother and father brought me back to damp, mortgaged England and I had to wear shoes for the first time, that those six years were something more: my benchmark for freedom, for generally doing

as I pleased. They are my lost domain, to which I daily want to return.

I have looked for it often in adult life, on desert islands, in mountains and ancient cities, and never found it. Then, last spring, at Luang Prabang, Laos's old royal capital, I brushed against its fences. Saturated in Buddhist tradition, the town's temples and French colonial-era villas snuggle into the junction of the Mekong and Nam Khan rivers like a spiritual Manhattan island, its atmosphere parcelled out in gusts of calm. In 1951 Norman

Left: Mekong delta in the early evening
Far left: Young monk in Luang Prabang

responsible for the state of immaterial serenity that envelops the town and, though their regime is severe (up at four, no food after midday), there is always a fresh supply of novices whose parents wish them raised in the 'way of the elders'. Theravada

'Yes, Nixon went to the moon and he thought Laos should look like that, so he bombed it until it did.'

After several days of sitting by the Mekong, visiting temples and inspecting lotuses in

The saffron-robed monks are responsible for the state of immaterial serenity that envelops the town

Buddhism goes on flourishing in Laos because it has been useful for its Communist leaders in preaching the spiritual benefits of poverty and providing an education that neither the state nor parents can afford otherwise.

It was these elements above all – the atmosphere of undisturbed pleasure, and the withdrawal from the temporal world signified by so many monks – that made Luang Prabang's haze and warm country air feel as enfolding as a Brisbane afternoon.

The day I arrived I walked up Mount Phousi, the sacred hill in the middle of town, and at the top secured spiritual credit by buying two tiny birds in a straw cage and releasing them. At six the evening came down softly – in fact the city rose gently to meet it – and the night market filled Sisavangvong Road.

Luang Prabang is also about letting go: I who flee after five minutes in Oxford Street became addicted over several evenings to the ribbons of stalls sequinned with the glitter of small lightbulbs. Low stools are provided to customers to examine the handwoven silk, silver and carving at road level. At the market's north end a half-dozen excellent Laotian-French restaurants wait.

The city's tranquillity has not erased memories of the violent past. On show at the royal palace is an audacious gift from President Nixon: a Laotian flag and a scale model of the Apollo 11 lunar module. Audacious because the gift was made in 1969 in the middle of a US offensive that dropped two million tons of bombs on north-eastern Laos. When I mentioned this artefact to a Lao silversmith he nodded.

roadside gardens – silent roads from which wheeled traffic is excluded – I found myself willing my state of pleasurable elevation and pampered serenity to last forever. I had, I thought, come close to re-entering that lost place of childhood. Perilously close. Urgently, I phoned my wife to check that she was still waiting for me. Luang Prabang is a place where I imagine young European men to be at extreme risk of spontaneously marrying a Laotian wife, abandoning ambition and settling to a life of modest commerce, six children and daily *pétanque* by the Mekong. It could be a happy destination. But not for me, or for anyone who has their lost domain, because for us the secret is not to find it again. When your life's work has been a never-ending search, you're not a finder but a searcher. You can never go back. Though, given the chance to relive Luang Prabang's glorious freedom and peace next year or the year after, I'd probably take it, to carry on looking.

Lewis wrote: 'It is the home-town of the siesta and the *Ultima Thule* of all French escapists in the Far East.' Luang Prabang manufactured its own tranquillity. After dinner with a French colonial administrator, 'the evening was rounded off by a routine visit to the local opium den, which, probably by design, was as decrepit and sinister as a waxworks exhibit. We stayed only a few minutes in this green-lit, melodramatic establishment ... One had to make some show of going to the devil.'

It is not accurate to describe Luang Prabang's appeal as preserved colonial charm – Laos has been a Communist state for more than thirty years – but graceful French villa architecture nestles down easily among the temples, and you still see Europeans in linen trousers stepping out of the odd postwar Mercedes onto deep-shaded restaurant terraces on Sisavangvong Road, invisible to the passing clusters of monks.

More than any other single influence, the saffron-robed monks are

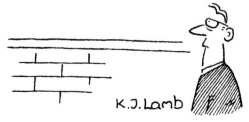

GOVERNMENT HEALTH WARNING

THE GOVERNMENT ISN'T VERY WELL

K.J.Lamb

Old Stagers

Ralph Richardson

RALPH RICHARDSON *achieved fame through sheer perseverance.* **PATRICK GARLAND** *remembers a celebrated and much-loved legend of stage and film*

'I always like to aim a little wide of the mark,' said Sir Ralph Richardson. He called me 'The Poet' as he did all directors, although in my opinion, directors are peculiarly unpoetic people.

Ralph was known for his benevolence and Sir John Gielgud once complained about his total inability to fathom the character of corruption when he was directing him as Macbeth – 'like several of his other tragic Shakespearean roles, a complete catastrophe.' At one of the rehearsals, a desperate Gielgud called out from the stalls: 'Oh Ralph, for goodness' sake, can't you be a little bit more beastly?'

Richardson tottered down to the edge of the stage and, addressing the shape of Gielgud in the auditorium, replied: 'Oh Johnny, I don't want to be beastly to anybody.'

There has never been anyone on the British stage remotely able to replace him and his peculiar brand of poetry, especially when playing rather mundane people, such as doctors or businessmen, and the magic he could bring to roles like Cyrano and Falstaff was legendary. But sometimes his eccentricity, which so endeared him to his fellow actors, was a disguise that concealed his

purposefulness, and in certain instances, his selfishness.

When he was a young actor, Ralph Richardson was taken on by an old-fashioned actor-manager by the name of Charles Doran, a member of a very distinguished traditional theatrical family. He reminisced one day about his early life in the theatre. Ralph told me how kind Doran had been to him when he was an absolute beginner and, frankly, not very good. Doran took on Ralph, imperfect and inept as he largely was, almost as a member of his family, staying together in digs not unlike those of Mr and Mrs Vincent Crummles. Time passed and Ralph fought his way steadily forwards with his curious indefinable quality, his personal magic, quite impossible to repeat or imitate, until he found his niche.

I visited Ralph in New York when he was appearing with John Gielgud in a very successful production of David Storey's elliptical play *Home*, directed by Lindsay Anderson. It received excellent notices from the critics of the *New York Times*, but completely baffled a Broadway audience more accustomed to musicals.

> **Ralph fought his way forwards with his curious indefinable quality until he found his niche**

I asked him how he succeeded in coping with incomprehension on the part of the audience for such a long period of time. Ralph reflected for a moment: 'In a way, my old friend Johnny Gielgud and I get on very well with the play, in spite of the audience not understanding a word of what we're talking about, but I must confess that every so often I get a passionate surge of emotion in my body, and I want to break away from the written text, and address my old friend Johnny Gielgud on the other side of the stage, and say to him: "Look here, this is all very well, but where have you hidden the diamonds, Mr Stacey?"'

His oddity took many forms. He was cast in the Sixties – rather appropriately, it must be admitted – in a black comedy by Joe Orton called *What the Butler Saw*. But when he performed at Brighton, where he was a much-loved celebrity, he was taken aback

Not beastly enough? Ralph Richardson as Macbeth with Margaret Leighton as Lady Macbeth in John Gielgud's 1952 production of *Macbeth*

by the audience's dislike of that sophisticated and indecent farce.

The play was not a success, and Ralph spent a lot of time in his hotel room, looking out to sea and writing letters of explanation and apology to a mass of reproachful theatre-goers who were demanding their money back. I heard it said with authority that Ralph often

He spent a lot of time in his room writing letters of apology to a mass of reproachful theatre-goers

used to send back a cheque from his own account for the sum of money demanded when the indignant letter contained torn-off ticket stubs. I was told that one evening in the middle of the performance he stepped forward unexpectedly to the front of the stage. He was playing a conventional doctor who spent much of the farce in a white coat, so he was a

'Is there a doctor in the house?' Ralph Richardson as Dr Rance in the 1969 production of *What the Butler Saw*, with Stanley Baxter (left) and Coral Browne

somewhat striking figure. Unscripted, he addressed the audience with the well-known cry, 'Is there a doctor in the house?' A voice called out from about the tenth row of the stalls, with hand upraised: 'Yes, Sir Ralph, I'm a doctor if you want one.' 'Oh, doctor,' Ralph replied in mournful tones. 'Isn't this a terrible play?'

OLDIE MASTERS
A guide to neglected artists
Vivian Forbes (1891–1937)

Ariadne (1937)
Ink and watercolour. 15 x 10 inches. Signed and dated.

IN THE MONTHS before Vivian Forbes's suicide following the unexpected death of his lover (the painter Glyn Philpott) the two painters exhibited work at the Redfern Gallery that, with hindsight, seems to prefigure the coming tragedy. Philpott's *Le Trayas* – a lonely, tomblike building above the deserted Mediterranean shore – and his *Two Muses at the Tomb of a Poet* are redolent of a melancholy symbolism that descends from Boecklin and Moreau. Forbes's series of Ariadne on the shore of Naxos watching Theseus sailing away from her also suggests a fascination with departure and loss.

Forbes had been a student of the older Philpott at the Chelsea Polytechnic and, although largely influenced by him, did produce a small, idiosyncratic body of oil paintings and watercolours of which this is typical.

Ann Barr and her parrot, Turkey, at home

Entertaining Miss Sloane

DAEMIENNE SHEEHAN *plays host to the grande dame*
of a unique West London social phenomenon

Every year Ann Barr, the creator and defender of the Sloane Ranger, coaxes her long-time companion, Turkey, an old African Grey parrot, out of depression after she has laid unfertilised eggs. During the last bout, Turkey secreted three eggs underneath the bath, where she vainly attempted to hatch them for forty days. Eventually, Ann lured Turkey out for an evening of British birdsong music and supper with our family, during which the parrot burst into opera. 'Turkey sings opera when she is really happy. Her first owners were opera singers. Turkey only stayed a year because every time they sang, she proved too much competition,' Ann affectionately observed.

The engine behind *The Sloane Ranger Handbook* is on top Sloane form, ensuring that everyone feels comfortable despite having a beady-eyed Turkey

perched on her back. Combining a peculiarly upper-class English courting of discomfort with a love of animals, Ann embodies good-natured Sloanish dignity as she sits at the table, wearing a tea cosy printed with dancing cats to keep that 'naughty bird' from pecking her ears.

Ann's mother hailed from a wealthy banking family and her father grew up in 'the lap of luxury' – as a young man he strolled through the streets of New York in 1925 with a leopard on a chain. Unlike her father, who had little interest in work, Ann proved to be more an industrious Sloane than a trust-fund ingénue: 'I was the only one who got a job. I couldn't bear the idea of being a spendthrift when people in our family depended on cheques from wealthier relatives.'

She co-wrote *TSRH* with Peter York, whom she had originally commissioned

to write an article on Sloane Rangers for *Harpers & Queen,* where she was features editor during the Seventies and Eighties; she says a sub, Martina Margetts, invented the term. York, who was keener on interviews than the retiring Ann, has often been credited as the book's sole author. It's a pity, Ann says, as 'he doesn't really like Sloanes. He's a social climber who wants to climb into a class that he doesn't even like. The book was about people I had grown up with – friends and family.'

She wrote the book to honour a younger sister, Dierdre Mulloy, who died of emphysema and 'showed me what a real Sloane Ranger was – their virtues of hard work, quiet loyalty and modesty. People like this keep the world running because they are willing to stay late to finish the work.

'I was the only one who stood up for Sloane Rangers at the time,' she continues. 'Everyone thought that they were boring people who sat on committees or loud, titled people. Sloanes are not titled, and they are the backbone of society. They care about what they do and don't like to overstep.' Appropriately enough, the original *TSRH* resembles a finishing-school deportment guide.

TSRH was published in 1982 during the height of Diana-mania. Although Diana, with a frosted shelf of hair, appeared on the front cover, Ann disputes her Sloane credentials. 'Diana was never modest,' she explains, 'and she

'All Sloane children are brought up on British Edwardian children's books'

completely lacked quiet loyalty.'

Many of *TSRH*'s gems were contributed by anonymous Sloanes and were developed into topics ranging from 'The Small Sloanes' Uniform' to 'China Restoration Courses'. Jokes such as 'Knobs take yobs' jobs' – referring to the then Sloane trend to take painting and decorating commissions – were printed alongside explanatory boxes, one of which began '"Colour Prejudice" – Navy (of course).'

Although Ann never married or had a family, she wrote the delightfully knowing box 'Your Books', which reads: 'The most crucial influences on Sloanes – even in the 1980s – are Edwardian. All Sloane children (of many nationalities all over the world, which make it cultural imperialism) are brought up on British Edwardian children's books ... Sloane mothers like the Edwardian pantheon in the battered handed-down books: they reinforce everything that is right. Many say things that one wouldn't

say out loud today. Those books strike the Sloane nerve: all the maids, dashing gents, common villains and Fauntleroy childhoods that radicals so hate. They do encourage your childishness: the unspoken belief that animals are people; that good things come in blue jackets; that every hill has a golden treasure inside it.'

Ann has now joined forces with a young fan, Will Staeton and is currently emeritus editor of the website, 'The Intrepid Fox'. The site, with its hushed reverence for all things Sloane, advises on social events and the best places to shop and eat. It is enlivened by Ann's own contributions, which are marked by acute social observation and maverick angles. A typical Ann feature explores how the Second World War changed Canadian polo.

I t is time for the recalcitrant Turkey to go to bed. 'Do come off my back, you naughty bird,' Ann pleads while gamely trying to shuffle her off with a giant feather duster. My husband, Wilde, suggests using the duster to shift her into the cage. It is a terrible error. Turkey, who has been making flirtatious birdie eyes at Wilde since she arrived, suddenly flies over to her quarry. The last thing Ann and I see is a terrified man and a green flash headed up the stairs. We hear mad running about above our heads and a door slams. Then Wilde reappears. 'I had no idea Turkey was on my back until I reached the top. I had to remove my shirt. She's up there now,' he pants.

'Remarkable,' a gently astonished Ann says. 'Your husband has come down bare-chested.' It is a point of etiquette not covered in the *TSRH*.

RANT

EMAILS ARE a barbaric intrusion into our civilisation. Millions are sent every day. It is like a virus.

They are destroying our post offices, creating a neurosis of false urgency and causing illiteracy in the young.

The three great communication inventions – telephone, fax and email – arrived in the wrong order. Telephone first, fax next and email last. Yet email is the most primitive. It needs a keyboard, a screen and you have to be able to type. Fax, you simply write or draw, drop it into a slot and press a button. Phone, and you speak to someone and they reply – live! It's called conversation.

Some people worship email. A bloke phoned me recently after we had missed one another several times. 'How can I contact you, Raymond? Have you got an email address?' 'Yes!' I screamed at him, 'but we're talking now, aren't we?'

Commuters get on the train at dawn and instead of reading the paper or doing the crossword, out come the laptops and work begins at 6.30 am. False urgency again. Emails also destroy conversation. People in open-plan offices email friends they can see across the room: 'c u pub 6?' I refuse to let the virus into the house. My assistant receives the tripe three miles away and every now and again, she cycles over with the latest red-hot emails in the basket on her handlebars. That's the way to do it! Civilisation.

RAYMOND BRIGGS

'Oh no! They've turned it into a Castropub!'

Ship of the Fens

*Each week the reprobate **WILFRED DE'ATH** pays a visit to Ely Cathedral
to recharge his spiritual batteries. Illustrations by **NICK BAKER***

On the short journey from Cambridge to Ely (14 minutes), I sit on the left side of the train in order to see the great cathedral, the Ship of the Fens, rising out of the early morning mist. It's best to arrive before 9 am, slipping in through a side door to avoid the snooty ladies trying to extract the entrance fee. As I have so often told them, I object to being made to Pay to Pray. Eventually, I protested to the Dean and he very kindly issued me with a free pass – for life.

I make the usual round of the side chapels, stopping in each to say a brief prayer and light a candle, but it is to the huge Lady Chapel that I am invariably drawn. Here one is at a pleasing distance from the turbaned chars hoovering and the choir practising and the organ booming. The startling statue of Our Lady, hovering over the altar as if in flight, is – well, it has to be said – sexy. She displays full, almost voluptuous, curves beneath her bright blue robe and her long hair is flaxen yellow. However, it is too early in the morning to allow her to distract me from my devotions...

Our wise old church has discovered that, if you behave and pray *as though* you believe, belief will be granted. In the Lady Chapel of Ely Cathedral I am learning this lesson anew. I go in on a mundane weekday morning feeling pretty agnostic and emerge twenty or thirty minutes later suffused with faith.

And so out into the nave, where, not long ago, I debated with the present Bishop of Rochester as to whether spirituality *per se* possesses any moral content. I said it didn't – it is morally neutral – and he said it *did*, but was kind enough to add that I was not without insight. I am, by then, on such a spiritual high that the rest of the time spent in the Cathedral tends towards the anti-climactic. Temptation to steal from the gift shop has entirely evaporated, as has the desire not to pay for the over-priced, inferior coffee in the refectory. I can't even be bothered to tell the grasping ladies what I really think of them. (The effects of the bad dreams

I go in on a mundane weekday morning feeling pretty agnostic and emerge suffused with faith

of the night before evaporate, too. I suffer, and have done for years, from nightmares of such evil that I have finally become convinced of the existence of their opposite, good, i.e. God. After my thirty minutes here, my spirit is cleansed.)

If I do have one complaint about the cathedral, it is that they *never* stop asking for money. I know they are obliged to make ends meet, but why can't they show a bit more faith that God will

The west tower of Ely Cathedral, left, and the nave, above

provide? At a choir concert there recently, the MC assured us that he would not, for once, be asking for any money. This was music to about a thousand ears, but at the end, of course, he did.

I emerge, refreshed, into the little town, which is really, like Wells, no more than a cathedral with a large village around it. There isn't a great deal to do in Ely, unless you visit Toppings, an excellent bookshop where they serve much better coffee than the cathedral's (for free) and where you can get books you can't get anywhere else, not even in Cambridge, whither I return in a much better frame of mind.

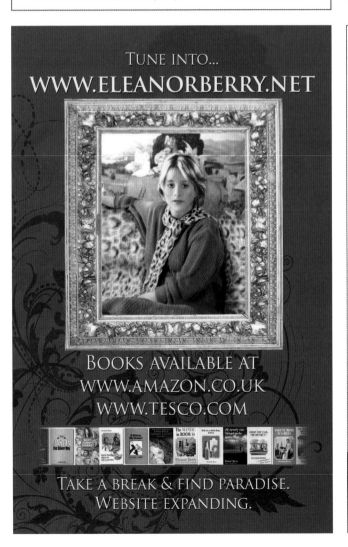